SPIRIT OF THE HORSE

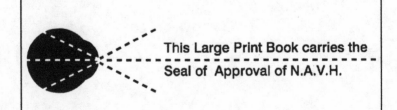

This Large Print Book carries the
Seal of Approval of N.A.V.H.

SPIRIT OF THE HORSE

A CELEBRATION IN FACT AND FABLE

WILLIAM SHATNER
WITH JEFF ROVIN

THORNDIKE PRESS
A part of Gale, Cengage Learning

GALE
CENGAGE Learning·

Farmington Hills, Mich • San Francisco • New York • Waterville, Maine
Meriden, Conn • Mason, Ohio • Chicago

GALE
CENGAGE Learning®

Copyright © 2017 by William Shatner.
Thorndike Press, a part of Gale, Cengage Learning.

ALL RIGHTS RESERVED
Thorndike Press® Large Print Popular and Narrative Nonfiction.
The text of this Large Print edition is unabridged.
Other aspects of the book may vary from the original edition.
Set in 16 pt. Plantin.

LIBRARY OF CONGRESS CATALOGING-IN-PUBLICATION DATA

Names: Shatner, William author. | Rovin, Jeff co-author.
Title: Spirit of the horse : a celebration in fact and fable / by William Shatner with Jeff Rovin.
Description: Large print edition. | Waterville, Maine : Thorndike Press, 2017. | Series: Thorndike press large print popular and narrative nonfiction
Identifiers: LCCN 2017016977 | ISBN 9781432839444 (hardcover) | ISBN 1432839446 (hardcover)
Subjects: LCSH: Horses—Literary collections. | Shatner, William. | Actors—Canada—Biography. | Large type books.
Classification: LCC PN6071.H73 S53 2017b | DDC 808.8/036296655—dc23
LC record available at https://lccn.loc.gov/2017016977

Published in 2017 by arrangement with Macmillan Publishing Group, LLC/St. Martin's Press

Printed in Mexico
1 2 3 4 5 6 7 21 20 19 18 17

I would like to dedicate this book to the wonderful animals I worked with, but I also need to mention the horses.

HORSES
All Glory
Beretta
Boston Legal
Call Me Ringo
Chic
Da Vinci
Eleanor Rigby
Lena
Lucy
Natasha
Revival
Sinatra
Sparkle
Spill the Ink
Sultan's Great Day
Time Machine
Tucker Belle

TRAINERS
Brett Day
Danny Gerardi
Joan Lurie
Raymond & Lillian Shively

CONTENTS

INTRODUCTION:
THE ZEN OF RISK

Most of us take some kind of risk or other. A new relationship; changing jobs; not studying as hard as we should for an exam; skydiving.

Of course, *some* of us are a little crazier than others.

If my life were a movie, or a TV series, what I'm about to tell you would be the precipitating event that caused me to look back at how I got here. Sort of like *Sunset Boulevard,* only without the swimming pool . . . and I'm also still alive!

Miraculously.

Since you're reading this book, you've already gathered that horses are a huge part of my life. They have been for more than thirty years. Without a doubt, horses are magnificent animals. Since almost everyone has seen one on-screen, or in a stable, or being ridden through city streets by a police officer, or even performing in a rodeo or a

11

circus, you know that already. Perhaps you've ridden one. But, as with most sports, there is also an inherent danger when riding.

I want to talk about that for a moment, the appeal of danger to me personally. It comes with the pro forma "Don't try this at home, kids."

When I do road races like the celebrity Grand Prix in which everybody is riding a powerful, souped-up vehicle and trying to kill each other — figuratively speaking, of course; it's more like bumper cars for thrill-seeking adults — I think, at 150 miles an hour, when I'm going into a right-hand turn, "Man, I'm going to lose it here." In that moment, I am euphoric. I took flying lessons where my opening class was conducted by this military adviser who put the plane in a tail-over-nose, wing-over-wing maneuver. You are, quite literally, tumbling in the air, and I thought, "I'm gonna die." In 2015, I partnered with *American Wrench* on TV for a cross-country motorcycle ride to benefit the American Legion. A 2,400-mile journey on a wonderful, custom-built but untested machine. Like a horse, there was a lot of power under my butt. A lot of that employed at high speeds on sharp turns that I wasn't always sure I could hold. But you never know until you try.

The bottom line is, I've been "going to die" at a variety of sports, from riding horses to racing cars. In fact, you drive high-performance cars with your ass, the way you drive a horse. Movement is felt in your butt and communicated to the rest of the body; it tells your arms, legs, and spine what to do and how to move. Which is a roundabout way of saying a good horseman will make a good driver. And vice versa . . . though, unlike cars, horses have a mind and will of their own and the musculature to enforce both.

We are, after all, talking about animals that can stand up to seventeen hands high — which is over five and a half feet and weigh on average slightly more than half a ton. Animals who are spirited *by nature.* That's a lot of strength and temperament to try to overcome. I try — I try hard, try diligently — to do that and am mostly successful. But not always.

The natural reaction of non–horse people, when I talk about some of the horse-riding accidents I've had, is, "Bill, why would any sane, reasonable person want to pursue this?" And they have a point. If I'm injured, acting is not something I can easily do from a hospital bed. But when you love something

— anything — sanity and practicality are not always your guiding principles.

And I love horses. As the poet says — let me count the ways!

This book was inspired by my desire not only to give my perspective on the excitement of the race and my love of horses, but to share the thoughts and experiences of others. I have selected some of my favorite equine nonfiction and fiction, myth and folktale, prose and verse. While all of these selections stand on their own as entertaining, informative, and/or quaint narratives, I have also written extensively about my own experiences to provide context for them. Together, I hope, these works will illuminate the experiences and joys, setbacks and triumphs of those who spend time in the company of horses.

THE FOUR-LEGGED OLYMPIAN

Horses are Olympic athletes. It's up to the rider to try to govern that power, that elegance, that perfection, that *will*. Failing that, failing to merge with and control that power, you're just a passenger. And a very vulnerable one at that.

I was on a beloved Saddlebred. Saddlebreds are descended from proud, spirited riding stock whose line dates back to the American Revolution. Hence the epithet "the Horse America Made."

The Saddlebred's nature is to be highly emotional, highly evolved, with lots of high-energy motion, a high neck — hell, everything *about* them is high. And it is the job of the rider and the trainer to channel all that energy into whatever performance the horse is supposed to give.

Now, some of these horses have all of those distinctive characteristics, only they are less highly charged. Or maybe they are a little slower for some other reason. As a result, they are sometimes made into Western Pleasure horses, animals known for their generally relaxed demeanor.

This particular horse I was riding was a really good example of that. I had purchased him because he had vital Saddlebred energy, but he didn't have enough motion in his legs. So I decided to make him into a Western Pleasure horse, because his beauty, and the motion of the legs that he *did* possess, could have made him a champion of that type, because a Western Pleasure horse has to walk, jog, and lope.

This particular horse was trained for two years by the Kentucky trainers whose job it is to handle these American Saddlebreds, to develop them to their full potential according to their breeding — which is to be show horses.

An essential part of this training is desensitization. This is an ongoing process. The trainer, the rider, both have to be extremely alert to new stimuli, to new and different things every day, at home or on the road. It might be a kind of bird or dog, it might be a crowd.

Think, for just a moment, about police horses and what they have to endure. Their trainers make noises, blow whistles, fire shots, break bottles, bang garbage cans, have people crowding around to make sure the horse is accustomed to these distractions. I saw some footage recently of the O. J. Simpson trial, when the crowd reacted to the jury's verdict outside the courthouse and the police horses were all lined up in case of trouble. Even with all their training, even with highly experienced police officers on their backs, as soon as the crowd erupted with this elemental shout, *all* the police horses shied. And several police officers almost came off their horses. For riders, this fundamental desensitization training is essential and very, very serious work.

After that basic desensitizing and training, this one horse eventually came to my Western trainer, Danny Gerardi, who trains all the Quarter Horses I own for reining — which is a sport that we'll get to later in the book. But the big difference is that reiners don't need to walk, jog, and lope: they need to gallop hard, slide to a stop, and do 180-degree turns. Fast turns and fast circles — the old, classic cowboy discipline, if you will.

One of the first things that needs to happen in this phase is that they have to be acclimatized in particular to horse shows, because stadiums and arenas, even a simple, ordinary stable, are filled with noise and strange things and beings. So we were at this one particular horse show where — in addition to all of the above — a parade on its way to the stadium goes right past the very stalls that our horses are in. With a little bit of preparation, not a problem. We have to close the stalls up and not let the horses see or hear the marching and floats and bands and the rest of the hubbub on its way to the venue. Understandably, if they get a glimpse of that parade it gets them excited and they start jumping around in their stalls.

So I'm on the back of this magnificent animal, comforting it, refamiliarizing it with me — and my hat blows off. When it comes to horses, you can factor in many things, you can *control* a bunch of them, but the wind doesn't fall in either category. Somebody went to pick up the hat and hand it to me. Well, as that is happening my Western Pleasure horse shies and I fall to the ground. I come off the horse. And it's all right because I wasn't hurt, just startled. I get back up, I get back on the horse, thinking, "Okay, that hat thing was unexpected."

If this had happened in a play, that would have been called "foreshadowing." If this had been a Greek play, Poseidon, the god of horses — more on him, later — would have been stroking his beard and chuckling behind the chorus.

The parade's done, the coast is clear, I go out, and now I'm riding this horse — walk, jog, and lope. And it's a *very* hot day. That's something you can't avoid. You react to that, instinctively: I went to wipe the perspiration off my forehead, not even thinking that it would disturb my hat. That inspired my Western Pleasure horse to whirl around so quickly that when I came off the horse — hard, this time — I was driven into the ground so roughly that I broke my leg. I felt it go, knew it at once, and I had to be rushed to the hospital. The only *good* thing was, I'd fallen enough by then to know how to do it, even though I was older. For example:

I was in competition in Louisville, Kentucky, and a young horse reared on me. Keep in mind, it's nothing like you see in the movies, where Zorro's horse Tornado goes back on his rear legs and stays there as Zorro waves at the camera while lightning flashes behind them. Uh-uh. This horse I was on reared and I began to fall over backward. Instinctively, I grabbed the reins to try to recover my seat. Instead, I succeeded in pulling the horse backward with me. Very un-Zorro-like. My initial thought — and you do have time to think, because the seconds slow to a surprising crawl — was that he was going to crush me. That's almost like having a Volkswagen Beetle roll over on you. (There's a scene in the film *How the West Was Won,* during the Cheyenne attack, where a horse and rider fall on an incline and the horse slowly rolls over the stuntman. Some things you just cannot anticipate.)

Anyway, everything is relative, right? I landed very, very hard, but "lucky" for me, in the last instant the horse went down to the side, and all he did was crush my leg. And then he got up, and he was fine, and I went to get up and I wasn't fine. I got up and I fell right back down.

As I'm lying there, kind of catching my breath and figuring out what to do next, a guy I didn't even know jumped on me, arms out like he was smothering a fire, and said, "Stay down, we're calling an ambulance." And I said, "Don't call an ambulance, I'll be okay." And he said, "You could be bleeding inside." And I lay back down and said, "Call an ambulance!"

Three good things came out of that accident. This isn't just a matter of me looking on the bright side of life, which I always try to do; they really were very, very positive.

The first benefit was that I learned how not to fall.

The second benefit was a visit with some wonderfully professional people at the Humana hospital in Louisville. They were very reassuring, in the best tradition of the medical profession, and it wasn't just because they were treating Captain Kirk. I had the time to watch them interact compassionately with everyone they cared for. I was grateful to hear that while I had some nerve damage it would be all right. And so it was.

The third benefit — speaking of Captain Kirk — is that the lesson of getting up and falling down, getting up and falling down, gave me the insight on how to play the death scene in *Star Trek Generations*. When the script called for me — *him* — to be shot in the back and he falls to the ground, I thought, "I'll just do what I did with the horse. I'll get up, I'll fall down, I'll get up, I'll fall down." So that's what I did. It was very effective. Art imitated life.

That's a recurring theme in this book. You're going to hear from some wonderful authors writing about our favorite animals, each of these authors having had different ideas, different experiences with horses.

TACHYHIPPODAMIA

BY WILLIAM J. POWELL (1872)

I could think of no better selection to begin our literary journey than an excerpt from this vintage guide on horse training. It is a seminal work of its kind.

This wonderful volume bears the ambitious subtitle *"GIVING FULL DIRECTIONS [ON] HOW TO BREAK AND RIDE COLTS; TO TAME THE MOST VICIOUS HORSES AND GENTLE THEM TO ALL KINDS OF VEHICLES OR WORK; TO BREAK THEM OF KICKING OR ANY OTHER BAD TRICKS; TO TEACH THEM ANY KINDS OF TRICKS OR ACTIONS; ETC., ETC. WITH NUMEROUS VALUABLE RECEIPTS FOR DISEASES OF HORSES, MULES, COWS, ETC.; HOW TO FATTEN HORSES, COWS, ETC., HOW TO TEACH TURKEYS AND ANIMALS TO DANCE, HOW TO TAME DEER, ETC., ETC."*

As in many works of its time and age, quite a few of the ideas herein have been modified or in some cases discredited. But it seems essential that we start our journey with a look back at what trainers were thinking in less enlightened times.

This work contains material attributed to John Solomon Rarey, himself the author of *The Complete Horse Tamer* (1862). Rarey is perhaps better known for the reference to him in Nicholas Evans's bestselling novel *The Horse Whisperer* (1995).

In *Tachyhippodamia* — which literally translates to "Rapid Horse Tame" — author Powell states that he first learned of a technique of breaking horses that had been conceived in the eighteenth century, most likely by the famed Irish trainer Daniel Sullivan, and he was determined to re-create and refine this skill. *Tachyhippodamia* was the result, and the technique can be summed up fairly as approaching the horse calmly so that it won't be afraid.

By the way, the "Drinnen" the author refers to in the text is Thomas Drinnen, a man whom Powell met in 1815 and of whom he wrote, "[He] appeared to me rather eccentric in some respects, but an active, intelligent man, and very fond of horses." Changing hats here to another life, I earnestly wish time travel were possible! It would have been wonderful to know men such as these, in a simpler, more rugged time. What fun, without the distraction of ever-present communications and social media, to have ridden the open plains with them!

This is a rather lengthy excerpt, one that I went over time and time again, trying to find something it could do without. I made a few gentle cuts, though each time, I found myself seduced by the innocent charms of its writing and ideas. I mean, "Cause your horse to be put into a small yard, stable or room. If in a stable or room, it ought to be a large one. . . ." Who dares to redact advice like that?

OBSERVATIONS UPON HORSES IN GENERAL: AND WHAT LED ME TO THE DISCOVERY OF BREAKING THEM IN A SHORT TIME.

The first experiments I made upon wild horses, in order to break them in a shorter time than that usually employed to that end, consisted in the application of different kinds of smells, such as opium, the oil of cumin, assafœtida, that callous substance called the spur which grows upon the inside of a horse's fore-legs, the sweat from a man's arm-pit, mare's milk, &c., &c. Opium has but little effect upon a horse, even if he smells it a considerable time. But of all these substances, no one tends so much to intoxicate, and even sicken, not only a horse but a man, as that taken from the horse when smelled of for any length of time. Any one who may doubt the veracity of what I here assert, can be easily convinced by experience, if he will. In the next place, the sweat from the arm-pit has a tendency to render a horse sleepy, if smelled for an hour or two. Some horses, thus rendered sleepy, can be handled; but on most horses it has no effect, or very little. Now, as I was determined to publish this secret some day or other, in its true light, I never revealed any other till now, but that accompanied with some one of these substances, with certain directions how to apply them. These directions contained enough of the true secret to tame a horse, so as to astonish the most penetrating. Now and then, a horse would remain gentle that had been thus tamed; but five out of ten would become wild again. Whenever I broke one myself, he always remained gentle. Drinnen sincerely thought that some of these substances were necessary to gentle a horse. I solemnly declare, before God and man, that I do not believe that a horse can be tamed, even for a short time, by the application of any of these substances, without applying to him more or less of the true secret; and furthermore: I declare, that all and every one of them are entirely useless, and of no effect. God is my witness, that if ever this secret was known before, I never learnt it from any man; I discovered it myself, and brought it, as I believe, to its greatest perfection.

A horse is gentled, by my secret, in from two to sixteen hours. The time I have most commonly employed, has been from four to six. We all know what pleasure it gives a parrot to have one scratch or rub him upon the head. Now, of the five senses, the sense of feeling possesses something more, as to its influence of materiality, than the other four. It has a similar effect upon animals as upon men. A horse feels a lively pain at the stroke of a whip, or the prick of a pin. He feels a pleasure in being curried, rubbed and handled. It is well known, that an object that frightens a horse, at first sight, will become familiar to him in a short time — even in a few minutes. The same may be said of those sounds which frighten him at first: such as the explosion of a gun or cannon; to all of which he soon becomes familiar, provided they are not accompanied with any thing that operates upon the sense of feeling; but he will never become familiar to the crack of a whip, so as not to be afraid of it, if he has been accustomed to experience its effects, when vigorously applied to his back. To conclude: Take away FEAR — Inspire CONFIDENCE — FAMILIARIZE.

THE SECRET.

"A GENTLE HAND MAY LEAD THE ELEPHANT BY A HAIR."

Cause your horse to be put into a small yard, stable or room. If in a stable or room, it ought to be a large one, in order to give him more exercise with the halter, before you lead him out. If the horse belongs to that class which appears only to fear man, you must introduce yourself gently into the stable, room or yard where the horse is. He will naturally run from you, and frequently turn his head from you; but you must walk about extremely slow and softly, so that he can see you, and whenever he turns his head towards you, which he never fails to do in a short time, say in a quarter of an hour, or half an hour — I never knew one to be much longer without turning towards me — at the very moment he turns his head, hold out your left hand towards him, and stand perfectly still, keeping your eyes upon the horse, and watching his motions, if he makes any. If the horse does not stir for ten or fifteen minutes, advance as slowly as possible, and without making the least noise, always holding out your left hand, without any other ingredient in it than what nature put in it. The reason of my having made use of certain ingredients before people — such as the sweat from under a man's arm, &c. — was, to disguise the real secret; and Drinnen, as well as several others, believed that the docility to which the horse arrived, in so short a time, was owing to those ingredients. It will be seen, in this explanation of the secret, that they were of no use, whatever; but, by placing so much confidence in them, those who had succeeded in breaking one horse, failed in another, and that is what I foresaw.

If the horse makes the least motion when you advance towards him, stop and stand perfectly still till he is quiet. Remain a few minutes in this position, and then advance again in the same slow, almost imperceptible manner. He generally keeps his eye steadfast on you, till you get nigh enough to touch him upon the forehead. When you are thus near to him, raise slowly, and by degrees, your hand, and let it come in contact with that part just above the nostrils, as lightly as possible. If the horse flinches, (as many will,) repeat with great rapidity those light taps or strokes upon the forehead, going a little further up towards his ears by degrees, and descending with the same rapidity, till he will let you handle his forehead all over. Then touch, in the same light manner, making your hands and fingers play around the bottom or lower part of the horse's ears, coming down, now and then, to his forehead, which may be looked upon as the helm that governs all the rest. Having succeeded in handling his ears, advance towards the neck with the same precautions, and in the same manner; observing always to augment the force of the strokes, whenever the horse will permit it. Perform the same on both sides of the neck, till he lets you take it in your arms without flinching. Proceed in the same progressive manner to the sides, and then to the back of the horse. From the tail come back again to the head; handle it well, as likewise the ears, neck, breast, &c., speaking now and then to the horse. Begin, by degrees, to descend to the legs, always ascending and descending, gaining ground every time you descend, till you get to his feet. Talk to the horse in Latin, Greek, French, English or Spanish, or in any other language you please, but let him hear the sound of your voice, which at the beginning of the operation is not quite so necessary, but which I have always done in making him lift up his feet: — "Hold up your foot," "Leve le pied" — "Alza el pie"

— "Aron ton poda," &c., at the same time lift his foot with your hand. He soon becomes familiar with the sounds, and will hold up his foot at command. Then proceed to the hind feet, and go on in the same manner; and, in a short time, the horse will let you lift them, and even take them up in your arms. All this operation is no magnetism, no galvanism. It is merely taking away the fear a horse generally has of a man, and familiarizing him with him, as the horse experiences a certain pleasure from this handling of him.

MY FIRST TIME

So there I was, having fallen . . . again. I was broken but unbowed, a man in the midst of a long, long love affair with horses. As with any love, you willingly take the pain that comes with it.

I *know* exactly where, when, and why the first blossom of that love appeared.

For many, naturally enough, their first exposure to horses was in the movies. Where else could most people even see moving, thundering horses except in a darkened theater? Whether it was Tom Mix or John Wayne, the horse enhanced an already great screen presence. And drama! Who could not be thrilled when, in 1938, Errol Flynn in *The Adventures of Robin Hood* leapt from the scaffold where he was about to be hanged, landed on the back of his horse, and made a getaway.

Yet, as much as those images fanned the flames for me, none of them was *the* seed. I actually had one contact with a real horse in my youth and it clearly got into my soul.

I was about twelve and we lived in the suburbs of Montreal, far enough out that there was empty land around, and on one of those pieces of land there was a stable. One day — and I forget how I actually got the money, though I think I told my parents I swabbed out the stables to ride the horse, which wasn't true but it made a nice story — anyway, one day I was able to wangle myself a ride on a rental horse. And I rode as though I'd been born in the saddle. I was neither afraid nor awkward, and people were commenting, "Oh, you ride well."

I remember thinking at the time: first, how much bigger I felt and how much smaller everything else seemed; second, how much power was beneath me, *tolerating* me (because I did have the sense that it could toss me any time I became a burden); and third, of course, how much I wanted to do it again.

I didn't get to do that for a long while, since it *was* a luxury and we didn't have the money for many of those . . . and if we did, it wasn't so I could ride a horse. But — I did say it was a seed, and the seed was planted.

When I told my mother, she wasn't angry but astonished. She asked, "Where did you learn to do that?" And I honestly didn't know, don't know. It was just a gift.

Or maybe it was some kind of time-spanning moment, where young me on horseback somehow connected with or had a glimpse of older me on horseback and realized: I'm destined to be back. I've lived long enough to believe that such things can and do happen!

EXPERIENCE OF TWO BOYS IN MANAGING HORSES, WITH MANY ANECDOTES OF QUADRUPEDAL INTELLIGENCE

Horse Stories and Stories of Other Animals,
BY THOMAS W. KNOX (1890)

You've got to love that title, and the short narrative that goes with it! Thomas Wallace Knox (1835–1896) was a well-known Civil War correspondent, who subsequently worked as a travel writer and historian. *Horse Stories* was part of his Boy Traveler series.

"Here's an account of how they break horses in Texas," said Mr. Graham, as he took up a newspaper, from which he proceeded to read as follows:

"There are but a few men who make it a business to break horses, and who possess sufficient skill and patience to conquer the fiery spirit of the most vicious animal. These 'wild horse riders,' as they are called, in addition to receiving the use of the horse while handling him, get fees ranging from five dollars to twenty-five dollars. Fearless Frank, a well-known Texas tamer, had been engaged to break a magnificent sorrel, called Mad Ranger. Ranger was a spoiled horse. He had been caught several times for the purpose of being saddled and bridled, but the tamers had been unable to do anything with him.

"The horse-lot was inclosed by massive logs and stout timbers, capable of successfully resisting the most determined effort on the part of the beasts to escape. Connected with the large enclosure were several smaller ones, and into one of these Ranger was driven. Frank then took from his saddle a coil of three-quarter-inch rope, forty feet long, and a second coil about half as long, but much heavier, and an oilcloth slicker. Thus equipped, he slipped into the inclosure and faced the horse. Making a noose in one of the coils, he quickly threw it over Ranger's head and fastened the other end to a post called the tug-post. The animal commenced to rear and plunge, but at every plunge the slack in the rope was taken up, and Ranger was soon alongside the post. Here he was made secure with a Spanish knot, which his struggles only served to tighten.

"Seizing the old slicker, the trainer next hit the horse over the head and neck, causing the animal to rear and kick. The horse was soon tired out, and the blows that fell upon him scarcely caused him to wince. The trainer next took his long rope and fastened it around Ranger's head in such a manner that it served as a halter. The other end of the rope was secured to the post. A rope was then placed around the animal's body in such a manner that it would not slip, and another rope was fastened to his hind foot. The rope attached to the foot was drawn through the one around his body and the end taken by the trainer.

"A couple of hard pulls brought the foot up to the stomach, and the horse was compelled to stand on three legs, thus unable to kick or rear. The trainer then patted the horse on the head and slipped the bridle on. Then the saddle was put in the proper place, and the stirrups 'hobbled,' to prevent any injury to the animal, should he fall. The rider then seated himself in the saddle, the ropes were taken from the horse's feet and body, the gate of the pen opened, and horse and rider dashed out on the prairie. For fully an hour the infuriated animal reared, plunged and jumped about, vainly endeavoring to throw his rider, but finally, becoming exhausted, came to a standstill, and had to be urged even to walk. It was then that the horse was broken."

"And now," said Mr. Graham, after pausing a moment, "did you ever hear of how they used to capture wild horses in Texas by 'creasing' them?"

"I've read about it," replied Charley, "but forget exactly how it was done."

"Well," responded Mr. Graham, "here's an account by a man who was once in the business and knows all about it. Shall I read it?"

Both the youths were anxious to hear about this manner of taking horses, whereupon their father gave them the following in the words of Mr. Hill, an experienced cattle raiser of Texas:

"In the early days of the cattle business in Texas, from 1857 to 1860, the ranges were overrun by bands of wild horses. These animals were a great nuisance, as they would get mixed with our loose horses and run them off when any one approached. As a rule, they were a rough, ill-shaped set of beasts, and almost untamable, so that few attempts were ever made to catch them, it being considered best to shoot them and thus get rid of a disturbing influence in our horse herds.

"Sometimes, however, a really fine animal would be seen and the ranchmen would try hard to secure it. But the ordinary mode of capture — lassoing — could seldom be used against wild horses, as these beasts were very shy, and even a poor horse, carrying no weight, could outstrip a very fine animal with a man on his back.

"In this extremity the Texans used to resort to a means of capturing the horses which is, I believe, exclusively American. It was discovered, I do not know how, that a blow upon a particular sinew in a horse's neck, located just above where the spine joins the skull, would paralyze the animal temporarily without doing it any permanent injury. In those days the Texans were nearly without exception fine shots, and at short range could send a rifle ball with phenomenal accuracy.

"The horses could not be approached on foot, and it was impossible to catch them on horseback. But, not to be overcome by any such difficulties, the cowboys discovered a way to capture them. Taking his rifle, a hunter would crawl through the thick chaparral until within fifty or sixty yards of the horse he desired to secure. Then, taking careful aim, he would endeavor to send a bullet through the top of the neck so as to strike the sinew. When this was properly done the horse would fall as if struck by lightning and remain insensible for ten or fifteen minutes, recovering completely in an hour or two, with no worse injury than a slight wound in the back of the neck that soon healed.

"The weapon universally employed in creasing mustangs was the old Hawkins rifle, which carried a bullet not much larger than a pea, had a set trigger and required but a small charge of powder. Hundreds of mustangs, always the best animals in the herd, used to be creased every year, and this practice was kept up until the herds had entirely disappeared.

"Some of the horses thus secured were very tough and fleet animals, but few were of any practical use. Nearly all were ir-reclaimably vicious, even when judged from the Texas standpoint. Even when broken to the saddle, they could only be ridden by the very best horsemen, and were always on the lookout to do their riders an injury. Strange to say, they seldom tried to kick, but a man had to be continually on the lookout for their fore feet and teeth. They only used their hind feet when a man was about to mount, but nearly every one of them had a trick of kicking forward as soon as the rider put his foot in the stirrup, and unless he was wary he would receive a terrible blow on the leg. I used to own a horse that, I believe, could scratch himself between the ears with his hind foot, his hind leg being apparently made of India rubber. The instant he felt a foot in the stirrup his hind hoof would come forward with the speed of lightning, in the attempt to inflict a most vicious kick. I gave up mounting him in the usual way and always used to vault into the saddle without touching the stirrups, a feat easily enough performed in my younger days, although I would have some difficulty in doing it now. I used to like to ride wild horses, but after one or two narrow escapes from their deadly fore feet, which they would use if a man carelessly stood in front of them, I gave it up and stuck to the tame stock."

Other stories about horses consumed the evening, and at length the boys said "Goodnight" and went to bed, where they doubtless dreamed of exciting experiences among the wild horses of Texas and other regions where those animals abound.

THE WINGED HORSE

For many of us, our first exposure to the idea of a flying horse was in books of Greek mythology and, in particular, tales of Pegasus. Though he's as old as any fictional being, there's a paradox: look up in the night sky today and you can see him, a northern constellation between Cygnus and Aquarius.

Other nations and other media have written about flying horses, and they have been memorably portrayed in films like Walt Disney's *Fantasia,* in 1940 — which had a Greco-Roman setting — and *Clash of the Titans* (1981), which depicted Pegasus himself, though the origin was somewhat altered.

So, why has Pegasus stood out and endured?

The Greeks were wonderful horsemen. They considered the horse a mystic, heroic part of life, a spiritual being as well as a means of conveyance and labor and an instrument of war. No other animal served so many domesticated functions across so wide a social spectrum, from pulling a plow to pulling a leader's chariot. Not surprisingly, the Greeks worshiped various iterations of the horse. Apollo, son of Zeus, pulled the sun through the sky in a flaming horse-drawn chariot. When Hades needed to leave the underworld, he did so on a horse made of shadows — the distaff side of Apollo's golden-skinned steeds. Ares, the god of war, rode fire-breathing stallions. Poseidon, the sea god, rode a chariot pulled by the Hippocampi, which were horses in the front, fishes in the back. There were the Wild Mares of Diomedes, a herd that attacked humans and were tamed by the hero Hercules as the eighth of his twelve legendary labors. There were also Centaurs, who had the heads and torsos of men but the bodies of horses (which we will talk about more, below); Hippalektryons, which were horses that had the hindquarters of roosters; and many others.

Yet Pegasus is the best known, and for very good reason. Whereas the mortal Icarus flew too close to the sun and perished, Pegasus had no such limitations. He became — and remains, some three thousand years later! — a symbol of the higher reaches of a sentient being. The higher reaches of the mind, of the spirit.

According to the myth, Pegasus was sired by Poseidon and his mother was Medusa. Some tales have it that the horse sprang from the blood of Medusa, which is wonderfully spiritual: Medusa was a Gorgon, a snake-headed monster, dark and bad: anyone who gazed directly at her turned to stone. That is, until the demigod Perseus used her reflection as a guide and lopped of her head with his sword. Now, these Greek tales, and the players in them, had multiple layers of meaning, so the idea here has always seemed to me that if we were able to overcome the evil in our nature, if we were able to slay it, then a higher being would arise — a flying horse springing from the dying womb of the Gorgon. And what lower symbol of human failure than a snake? He was there in the Garden of Eden, after all, helping us to spoil it.

As I think about this, and how it relates to my own experience playing Captain Kirk, it occurs to me that, though he didn't ride a winged horse named Pegasus, Kirk did fly through space and fight various battles. You can make the argument that the starship *Enterprise* was a metaphor for horses of all times and every location — riding that vehicle, that means of transportation, into the sunset, into the unknown like we did across the West and depending on it for survival. In fact, speaking of archetypes, we had an episode in the second season of *Star Trek,* "Who Mourns for Adonais?," where the crew is captured by an alien who says he's the aforementioned sun god Apollo. That episode posited a temple as the source of his powers — a fun way for a show about future heroic explorers to pay homage to their ancient historic and mythic roots.

I have no idea if our journeys that week took us through the constellation Pegasus. I would like to believe that was written in the stars.

PEGASUS, THE HORSE WHO COULD FLY

Wonder Stories: The Best Myths for Boys and Girls,
BY CAROLYN SHERWIN BAILEY (1920)

Ms. Bailey was a well-known children's-book author of the first half of the twentieth century, and one of her works, *Miss Hickory,* won the prestigious Newbery Medal for 1947.

She tells the old tale of Pegasus in her characteristically charming way.

A very strange thing happened when Perseus so heroically cut off the head of Medusa, the Gorgon. On the spot where the blood dripped into the earth from Perseus' sword there arose a slender limbed, wonderful horse with wings on his shoulders. This horse was known as Pegasus, and there was never, before or since, so marvelous a creature.

At that time, a young hero, Bellerophon by name, made a journey from his own country to the court of King Iobates of Lycia. He brought two sealed messages in a kind of letter of introduction from the husband of this king's daughter, one of

Bellerophon's own countrymen. The first message read,

"The bearer, Bellerophon, is an unconquerable hero. I pray you welcome him with all hospitality."

The second was this,

"I would advise you to put Bellerophon to death."

The truth of the matter was that the son-in-law of King Iobates was jealous of Bellerophon and really desired to have him put out of the way in order to satisfy his own ambitions.

The King of Lycia was at heart a friendly person and he was very much puzzled to know how to act upon the advice in the letter introducing Bellerophon. He was still puzzling over the matter when a dreadful monster, known as the Chimaera, descended upon the kingdom. It was a beast far beyond any of mortal kind in terror. It had a goat's rough body and the tail of a dragon. The head was that of a lion with wide spreading nostrils which breathed flames and a gaping throat that emitted poisonous breath whose touch was death. As the subjects of King Iobates appealed to him for protection from the Chimaera a sudden thought came to him. He decided to send the heroic stranger, Bellerophon, to meet and conquer the beast.

The hero had expected a period of rest at the court of Lycia. He had looked forward to a feast that might possibly be given in his honor and a chance to show his skill in throwing the discus and driving a chariot at the court games. But the day after Bellerophon arrived at the palace of King Iobates, he was sent out to hunt down and kill the Chimaera.

He had not the slightest idea where he was to go, and neither had he any plan for destroying the creature, but he decided that it would be a good plan to spend the night in the temple of Minerva before he met the danger face to face. Minerva was the goddess of wisdom and might give him help in his hopeless adventure.

So Bellerophon journeyed to Athens, the chosen city of Minerva, and tarried for a night in her temple there, so weary that he fell asleep in the midst of his supplications to the goddess. But when he awoke in the morning, he found a golden bridle in his hands, and he heard a voice directing him to hasten with it to a well outside of the city.

Bellerophon took the golden reins firmly in his hand.

Pegasus, the winged horse, had been

pasturing meanwhile in the meadows of the Muses. There were nine of these Muses, all sisters and all presiding over the arts of song and of memory. One took care of poets and another of those who wrote history. There was a Muse of the dance, of comedy, of astronomy, and in fact of whatever made life more worthwhile in the sight of the gods. They needed a kind of dream horse like Pegasus with wings to carry them on his back to Mount Olympus whenever they wanted to return from the earth.

Bellerophon had never known of the existence even of Pegasus, but when he reached the well to which the oracle had directed him, there stood Pegasus, or, rather, this horse of the Muses poised there, for his wings buoyed him so that his hoofs could scarcely remain upon the earth. When Pegasus saw the golden bridle that the goddess of Wisdom had given Bellerophon, he came directly up to the hero and stood quietly to be harnessed. A dark shadow crossed the sky just then; the dreaded Chimaera hovered over Bellerophon's head, its fiery jaws raining sparks down upon him.

Bellerophon mounted upon Pegasus and took the golden reins firmly in one hand as he brandished his sword in the other. He rose swiftly in the air and met the ravening creature in a fierce battle in the clouds. Not for an instant did the winged horse falter, and Bellerophon killed the Chimaera easily. It was a great relief to the people of Lycia, and indeed to people of all time. You may have heard of a Chimaera. It means nowadays any kind of terror that is not nearly so hard to conquer as it seemed in the beginning when people were afraid of it.

This story ought to end with the hero returning his winged steed to the Muses and entering the kingdom of Lycia in great triumph, but something very different happened. Bellerophon decided to keep Pegasus, and he rode him so long and so hard that he grew very full of pride and presumption in his success. One day Bellerophon made up his mind to drive Pegasus to the gates of the gods in the sky which was too great an ambition for a mortal who had received no invitation as yet from the dwellers on Mount Olympus. Jupiter saw this rider of the skies mounting higher and higher and he became very angry with him. He sent a gadfly which stung Pegasus and made him throw Bellerophon to the earth. He was always lame and blind after that.

It really had not been the fault of Pegasus at all. He was only the steed of those who followed dreams, even if he did have wings.

When his rider fell, Pegasus fell too, and he landed unhurt but a long distance from his old pastures. He did not know in which direction they lay or how to find the road that led back to his friends, the Muses. Pegasus' wings seemed to be of no use to him. He roamed from one end of the country to the other, driven from one field to the next by the rustics who mistook him for some sort of a dragon because of his wings. He grew old and lost his fleetness. It even seemed to him that his wings were nothing but a dragging weight and that he would never be able to use them again.

Finally the same thing happened to Pegasus that happens to old horses to-day that have enjoyed a wonderful youth as racers. He was sold to a farmer and fastened to a plough.

Pegasus was not used to this heavy work of the soil; his strength was better suited to climbing through the air than plodding along the surface of the earth. He used all the strength he could put forth in pulling the plough, but his wings dragged and were in the way and his master beat his aching back with an ox whip. That might have been the end of this winged horse, but one day good fortune came to him.

There was a youth passing by who was

beloved of the Muses. He was so poor that he had often no other shelter than the woods and hedges afforded, or any food save wild fruits and the herbs of the field. But this youth could put the beauties of the earth, its hills and valleys, its temples, flowers, and the desires and loves of its people into words that sang together as the notes of a lute sang. He was a young poet.

The poet felt a great compassion for the horse he saw in the field, bent low under the blows of his clownish master, and with wings dragging and tattered.

"Let me try to drive your horse," he begged, crossing the field and mounting upon Pegasus' back.

It was suddenly as if one of the gods were riding Pegasus. He lifted his head high, and his heavy feet left the clods of earth. His wings straightened and spread wide. Carrying the youth, Pegasus arose through the air as the country people gathered from all the neighboring farms to watch the wonder, a winged horse with a flowing golden mane rising and then hidden within the clouds that opened upon Mount Olympus.

THE HORSE AND THE OLIVE

Old Greek Stories,
BY JAMES BALDWIN (1895)

"Greek mythology" is a very broad term used to describe a vast body of religious and secular stories that are thousands of years old. Like the best stories, this one tells us as much about ourselves as it does about the topic. Interestingly, Mr. Baldwin chose to use the better-known Roman name for the god Poseidon, which was Neptune — though the name of the Greek goddess Athena is intact.

By the way, author Baldwin wrote dozens of children's books and is not to be confused with the African-American author who wrote *Go Tell It on the Mountain* and other classic works.

I. FINDING A KING.

On a steep stony hill in Greece there lived in early times a few very poor people who had not yet learned to build houses. They made their homes in little caves which they dug in the earth or hollowed out among the rocks; and their food was the flesh of wild animals, which they hunted in the woods, with now and then a few berries or nuts. They did not even know how to make bows and arrows, but used slings and clubs and sharp sticks for weapons; and the little clothing which they had was made of skins. They lived on the top of the hill, because they were safe there from the savage beasts of the great forest around them, and safe also from the wild men who sometimes roamed through the land. The hill was so steep on every side that there was no way of climbing it save by a single narrow footpath which was always guarded by some one at the top.

One day when the men were hunting in the woods, they found a strange youth whose face was so fair and who was dressed so beautifully that they could hardly believe him to be a man like themselves. His body was so slender and lithe, and he moved so nimbly among the trees, that they fancied him to be a serpent in the guise of a human being; and they stood still in wonder and alarm. The young man spoke to them, but they could not understand a word that he said; then he made signs to them that he was hungry, and they gave him something to eat and were no longer afraid. Had they been like the wild men of the woods, they might have killed him at once. But they wanted their women and children to see the serpent man, as they called him, and hear him talk; and so they took him home with them to the top of the hill. They thought that after they had made a show of him for a few days, they would kill him and offer his body as a sacrifice to the unknown being whom they dimly fancied to have some sort of control over their lives.

But the young man was so fair and gentle that, after they had all taken a look at him, they began to think it would be a great pity to harm him. So they gave him food and treated him kindly; and he sang songs to them and played with their children, and made them happier than they had been for many a day. In a short time he learned to talk in their language; and he told them that his name was Cecrops, and that he had been shipwrecked on the seacoast not far away; and then he told them many strange things about the land from which he had come and to which he would never be able to return. The poor people listened and wondered; and it was not long until they began to love him and to look up to him as one wiser than themselves. Then they came to ask him about everything that was to be done, and there was not one of them who refused to do his bidding.

So Cecrops — the serpent man, as they still called him — became the king of the poor people on the hill. He taught them how to make bows and arrows, and how to set nets for birds, and how to take fish with hooks. He led them against the savage wild men of the woods, and helped them kill the fierce beasts that had been so great a terror to them. He showed them how to build houses of wood and to thatch them with the reeds which grew in the marshes. He taught them how to live in families instead of herding together like senseless beasts as they had always done before. And he told them about great Jupiter and the Mighty Folk who lived amid the clouds on the mountain top.

II. CHOOSING A NAME.

By and by, instead of the wretched caves among the rocks, there was a little town on the top of the hill, with neat houses and a market place; and around it was a strong wall with a single narrow gate just where the footpath began to descend to the plain. But as yet the place had no name.

One morning while the king and his wise men were sitting together in the market place and planning how to make the town become a rich, strong city, two strangers were seen in the street. Nobody could tell how they came there. The guard at the gate had not seen them; and no man had ever dared to climb the narrow footway without his leave. But there the two strangers stood. One was a man, the other a woman; and they were so tall, and their faces were so grand and noble, that those who saw them stood still and wondered and said not a word.

The man had a robe of purple and green wrapped round his body, and he bore in one hand a strong staff with three sharp spear points at one end. The woman was not beautiful, but she had wonderful gray eyes; and in one hand she carried a spear and in the other a shield of curious workmanship.

"What is the name of this town?" asked the man.

The people stared at him in wonder, and hardly understood his meaning. Then an old man answered and said, "It has no name. We who live on this hill used to be called Cranae; but since King Cecrops came, we have been so busy that we have had no time to think of names."

"Where is this King Cecrops?" asked the woman.

"He is in the market place with the wise

men," was the answer.

"Lead us to him at once," said the man.

When Cecrops saw the two strangers coming into the market place, he stood up and waited for them to speak. The man spoke first:

"I am Neptune," said he, "and I rule the sea."

"And I am Athena," said the woman, "and I give wisdom to men."

"I hear that you are planning to make your town become a great city," said Neptune, "and I have come to help you. Give my name to the place, and let me be your protector and patron, and the wealth of the whole world shall be yours. Ships from every land shall bring you merchandise and gold and silver; and you shall be the masters of the sea."

"My uncle makes you fair promises," said Athena; "but listen to me. Give my name to your city, and let me be your patron, and I will give you that which gold cannot buy: I will teach you how to do a thousand things of which you now know nothing. I will make your city my favorite home, and I will give you wisdom that shall sway the minds and hearts of all men until the end of time."

The king bowed, and turned to the people, who had all crowded into the market place.

"Which of these mighty ones shall we elect to be the protector and patron of our city?" he asked. "Neptune offers us wealth; Athena promises us wisdom. Which shall we choose?"

"Neptune and wealth!" cried many.

"Athena and wisdom!" cried as many others.

At last when it was plain that the people could not agree, an old man whose advice was always heeded stood up and said:

"These mighty ones have only given us promises, and they have promised things of which we are ignorant. For who among us knows what wealth is or what wisdom is? Now, if they would only give us some real gift, right now and right here, which we can see and handle, we should know better how to choose."

"That is true! That is true!" cried the people.

"Very well, then," said the strangers, "we will each give you a gift, right now and right here, and then you may choose between us."

Neptune gave the first gift. He stood on the highest point of the hill where the rock was bare, and bade the people see his power. He raised his three-pointed spear high in the air, and then brought it down with great force. Lightning flashed, the earth shook, and the rock was split half way down to the bottom of the hill. Then out of the yawning crevice there sprang a wonderful creature, white as milk, with long slender legs, an arching neck, and a mane and tail of silk.

The people had never seen anything like it before, and they thought it a new kind of bear or wolf or wild boar that had come out of the rock to devour them. Some of them ran and hid in their houses, while others climbed upon the wall, and still others grasped their weapons in alarm. But when they saw the creature stand quietly by the side of Neptune, they lost their fear and came closer to see and admire its beauty.

"This is my gift," said Neptune. "This animal will carry your burdens for you; he will draw your chariots; he will pull your wagons and your plows; he will let you sit on his back and will run with you faster than the wind."

"What is his name?" asked the king.

"His name is Horse," answered Neptune.

Then Athena came forward. She stood a moment on a green grassy plot where the children of the town liked to play in the evening. Then she drove the point of her spear deep down in the soil. At once the air was filled with music, and out of the earth there sprang a tree with slender branches and dark green leaves and white flowers and violet green fruit.

"This is my gift," said Athena. "This tree will give you food when you are hungry; it will shelter you from the sun when you are faint; it will beautify your city; and the oil from its fruit will be sought by all the world."

"What is it called?" asked the king.

"It is called Olive," answered Athena.

Then the king and his wise men began to talk about the two gifts.

"I do not see that Horse will be of much use to us," said the old man who had spoken before. "For, as to the chariots and wagons and plows, we have none of them, and indeed do not know what they are; and who among us will ever want to sit on this creature's back and be borne faster than the wind? But Olive will be a thing of beauty and a joy for us and our children forever."

"Which shall we choose?" asked the king, turning to the people.

"Athena has given us the best gift," they all cried, "and we choose Athena and wisdom!"

"Be it so," said the king, "and the name of our city shall be Athens."

From that day the town grew and spread,

and soon there was not room on the hilltop for all the people. Then houses were built in the plain around the foot of the hill, and a great road was built to the sea, three miles away; and in all the world there was no city more fair than Athens.

In the old market place on the top of the hill the people built a temple to Athena, the ruins of which may still be seen. The olive tree grew and nourished; and, when you visit Athens, people will show you the very spot where it stood. Many other trees sprang from it, and in time became a blessing both to Greece and to all the other countries round the great sea. As for the horse, he wandered away across the plains towards the north and found a home at last in distant Thessaly beyond the River Peneus. And I have heard it said that all the horses in the world have descended from that one which Neptune brought out of the rock; but of the truth of this story there may be some doubts.

The Horse, Hunter, and Stag

The Aesopica (Aesop's Fables)

The Greek myths were told and retold, and were not written down for many millennia. When they were, they were still recited with many variations, some large, some minor.

I was astonished to discover that we know so little about one of the best-known storytellers in world history. Aesop was a slave who lived in the fifth century BCE in Greece. That's it! We're not even sure whether he actually invented the stories that are attributed to him, only popularized them, or both.

Aesop told and retold dozens of "fables" — short stories with a moral lesson — which featured "anthropomorphic" animals, meaning they walked and talked like people. And in their very human personalities, they were instantly recognizable as people the listeners knew . . . and could learn from. Like this headstrong horse. . . .

A quarrel had arisen between the Horse and the Stag, so the Horse came to a Hunter to ask his help to take revenge on the Stag. The Hunter agreed, but said: "If you desire to conquer the Stag, you must permit me to place this piece of iron between your jaws, so that I may guide you with these reins, and allow this saddle to be placed upon your back so that I may keep steady upon you as we follow after the enemy."

The Horse agreed to the conditions, and the Hunter soon saddled and bridled him. Then with the aid of the Hunter the Horse soon overcame the Stag, and said to the Hunter: "Now, get off, and remove those things from my mouth and back."

"Not so fast, friend," said the Hunter. "I have now got you under bit and spur, and prefer to keep you as you are at present."

Moral: If you allow men to use you for your own purposes, they will use you for theirs.

THE WORLD IS A CAROUSEL

Flying horses are everywhere. In Norse mythology, for example, Hófvarpnir was the name of the steed that was ridden by Gná, the goddess of the breeze. They galloped through air and over the seas whenever she was sent on an errand by the goddess Frigg, wife of Odin — king of the gods. In fact, the name itself means "One Who Tosses His Hooves." Pretty much everything we know about Hófvarpnir comes from two small passages in the Icelandic writer Snorri Sturluson's sprawling saga, *Prose Edda* . . .

'Mikä siellä lentää, mikä siellä kulkee ja ilman läpi liukuu?'

'En lennä, kumminkin kuljen ja liu'un ilman halki Hófvarpnir-hevosellani, jonka Hamskerpir sai Gardrofa'n kanssa.'

Which, according to scholar Jesse Byock, translate as:

"What flies there?
What fares there?
or moves through the air?"

"I fly not
though I fare
and move through the air
on Hófvarpnir
the one whom Hamskerpir got
with Gardrofa."

If there is a fanciful horse that comes close to rivaling the enduring popularity and symbolism of the flying horse, it is the Centaur — half man, half horse. Centaurs, along with their female counterparts, Centaurides, are known primarily from Greek mythology. That has to do with the wide dissemination of the Greek tales throughout Europe. Adapting them, the Romans helped to codify many of these tales.

However, not just the Greek but many cultures, in every age, had a reverent approach to the horse — from the Japanese to the Native Americans. Like the Greeks, they used them in war, they used them in peace, and they had statues of them. They worshiped them in body and spirit.

In fact, an interesting anecdote. Some Japanese warriors — among others — fashioned saddles that were as crude as a sheepskin lashed to the back of a horse, so you were essentially riding bareback and only occasionally with something that passed for stirrups. I was in Japan and I got on a horse that was trained and owned by Japanese entertainers who would put on a horse show, showing how the Japanese soldiers mounted and fought on horseback in the days when there were these fiefdoms and the saddle barely existed, and the horse was half wild.

I got on and off very quickly — much to my chagrin, because I really wanted to experience this. But I didn't trust the saddle and, more importantly, I trusted the horse even less.

Regardless of the saddle, regardless of the country, that image of a horseman straddling a mount represented the ultimate power of the human being in a nontechnological age. The rider's size and innate ability was joined and amplified by the horse's stature and ability.

It is said that in the Minoan/Aegean world, nomads were mounted on horses, which was something strange to the non-riding cultures they encountered. And as they approached, either in the half-light or the desert reflections, they appeared as half man, half animal. The Aztecs apparently had a similar fear and wonderment about the Spanish cavalry. Such sightings, in far distant times, were probably not just the origin of the myths, they are rooted in something as old as civilization, something that is so deeply bound in the human psyche that it's almost inextricable. Something so atavistic yet fitting that we had to create myths to personify an ecstatic, almost preternatural relationship that is otherwise inexplicable.

Poets have struggled to accomplish as much with love and sex throughout the millennia. At least the horse is somewhat consistent.

My own sleep is sometimes filled with Centaur-like imagery of being one with the horse. It will start with me atop the horse galloping across the field, the horse's head visible ahead, his eyes becoming my eyes as if it were me galloping. This may be a Freudian concept embedded in our subconscious, as I suggested above. Perhaps our genetic memory knows something that anthropologists do not — that we arose from a common ancestor, recently enough for it to be there, still, in our DNA.

I wonder, though, if there may be something else at work, something less grandiose or perhaps working in tandem with pantheism. Perhaps there's a very practical way to explain these ancient stories and ideas, at least in some cultures. Perhaps they were designed to be tutorial. I've had feelings of being united with the horse because as you get older your legs are less fast, and you don't run or even walk as well as you did. But when you are on horseback, the power is yours again — greater than in your youth. In a way you are greater than youth, because you have wisdom, an inner tranquility that allows you to merge with the horse.

In later years I have had dreams of the horse and me being one, and I'm running and the horse is running and it's all the same. Perhaps it is from the subconscious desire to be greater than what we are that the idea of the Centaur emerged.

Most likely, it is all of the above.

As evidence, I offer the *púca* or pooka, a shape-changing Irish spirit that was either a black horse, a goat, or a rabbit. They were infamous for bringing bad luck to whoever they came in contact with. I've found, in various tales, that they could assume human form but always with some part of the animal still present: bunny ears, a goat's beard, a horse's tail. Now, it would seem odd that the Irish would select three creatures that we generally perceive as docile to be demonic. Why would they have come up with this?

I believe it is symbolic. The stories can be traced back to the Norse and I believe that the idea is simple: any peaceful animal, any animal that has no dark, conniving features, can be corrupted by a human or by human interaction.

As equestrians, we always hope that the best qualities of horse and rider are united. A union of what Daoism calls our good and "authentic nature" can only produce a better whole.

THE FOX AND THE HORSE

Children's and Household Tales,
BY THE BROTHERS GRIMM (1812)

The remarkable brothers Jacob (1785–1863) and Wilhelm Grimm (1786–1859) are probably the best known and most widely read fairy tale anthologists in the world. They were German scholars, linguists, and authors whose avocation was collecting and writing down folklore. So much of this material was spoken — told around the hearth by parents to children, and then to their children — that the brothers feared at some point it would be lost if they didn't write it down. Many stories were so characteristic of local culture that the brothers wanted them to be preserved to showcase the minds and hearts of the people. Among the stories they gave to the world were "Hansel and Gretel," "Cinderella," "Rapunzel," "Sleeping Beauty," "Rumpelstiltskin," "Snow White," and the one below.

A peasant once had a faithful Horse, but it had grown old and could no longer do its work. Its master grudged it food, and said: "I can't use you any more, but I still feel kindly towards you, and if you show yourself strong enough to bring me a Lion I will keep you to the end of your days. But away with you now, out of my stable"; and he drove it out into the open country.

The poor Horse was very sad, and went into the forest to get a little shelter from the wind and weather. There he met a Fox, who said: "Why do you hang your head, and wander about in this solitary fashion?"

"Alas!" answered the Horse, "avarice and honesty cannot live together. My master has forgotten all the service I have done him for these many years, and because I can no longer plough he will no longer feed me, and he has driven me away."

"Without any consideration?" asked the Fox.

"Only the poor consolation of telling me that if I was strong enough to bring him a Lion he would keep me, but he knows well enough that the task is beyond me."

The Fox said: "But I will help you. Just you lie down here, and stretch your legs out as if you were dead." The Horse did as he was told, and the Fox went to the Lion's den, not far off, and said: "There is a dead Horse out there. Come along with me, and you will have a rare meal." The Lion went with him, and when they got up to the Horse, the Fox said: "You can't eat it in comfort here. I'll tell you what. I will tie it

71

to you, and you can drag it away to your den, and enjoy it at your leisure."

The plan pleased the Lion, and he stood quite still, close to the Horse, so that the Fox should fasten them together. But the Fox tied the Lion's legs together with the Horse's tail, and twisted and knotted it so that it would be quite impossible for it to come undone.

When he had finished his work he patted the Horse on the shoulder, and said: "Pull, old Grey! Pull!"

Then the Horse sprang up, and dragged the Lion away behind him. The Lion in his rage roared, so that all the birds in the forest were terrified, and flew away. But the Horse let him roar, and never stopped till he stood before his master's door.

When the master saw him he was delighted, and said to him: "You shall stay with me, and have a good time as long as you live."

And he fed him well till he died.

THE BLACK HORSE

More Celtic Fairy Tales,
BY JOSEPH JACOBS (1895)

In his preface, Mr. Jacobs, an English anthologist, indicates that most of the tales — like those of the Brothers Grimm — belong to regional antiquity, their origins unknown and unknowable.

The "garron" referred to in this story is a small but sturdy workhorse.

Once there was a king and he had three sons, and when the king died, they did not give a shade of anything to the youngest son, but an old white limping garron.

"If I get but this," quoth he, "it seems that I had best go with this same."

He was going with it right before him, sometimes walking, sometimes riding. When he had been riding a good while he thought that the garron would need a while of eating, so he came down to earth, and what should he see coming out of the heart of the western airt towards him but a rider riding high, well, and right well.

"All hail, my lad," said he.

"Hail, king's son," said the other.

"What's your news?" said the king's son.

"I have got that," said the lad who came. "I am after breaking my heart riding this ass of a horse; but will you give me the limping white garron for him?"

"No," said the prince; "it would be a bad business for me."

"You need not fear," said the man that came, "there is no saying but that you might make better use of him than I. He has one value, there is no single place that you can think of in the four parts of the wheel of the world that the black horse will not take you there."

So the king's son got the black horse, and he gave the limping white garron.

Where should he think of being when he mounted but in the Realm Underwaves. He went, and before sunrise on the morrow he was there. What should he find when he got there but the son of the King Underwaves holding a Court, and the people of the realm gathered to see if there was any one who would undertake to go to seek the daughter of the King of the Greeks to be the prince's wife. No one came forward, when who should come up but the rider of the black horse.

"You, rider of the black horse," said the prince, "I lay you under crosses and under spells to have the daughter of the King of the Greeks here before the sun rises to-morrow."

He went out and he reached the black horse and leaned his elbow on his mane, and he heaved a sigh.

"Sigh of a king's son under spells!" said the horse; "but have no care; we shall do the thing that was set before you." And so off they went.

"Now," said the horse, "when we get near the great town of the Greeks, you will notice that the four feet of a horse never went to the town before. The king's daughter will see me from the top of the castle looking out of a window, and she will not be content without a turn of a ride upon me. Say that she may have that, but the horse will suffer no man but you to ride before a woman on him."

They came near the big town, and he fell to horsemanship; and the princess was looking out of the windows, and noticed the horse. The horsemanship pleased her, and she came out just as the horse had come.

"Give me a ride on the horse," said she.

"You shall have that," said he, "but the horse will let no man ride him before a woman but me."

"I have a horseman of my own," said she.

"If so, set him in front," said he.

Before the horseman mounted at all, when he tried to get up, the horse lifted his legs and kicked him off.

"Come then yourself and mount before me," said she; "I won't leave the matter so."

He mounted the horse and she behind him, and before she glanced from her she was nearer sky than earth. He was in Realm Underwaves with her before sunrise.

"You are come," said Prince Underwaves.

"I am come," said he.

"There you are, my hero," said the prince. "You are the son of a king, but I am a son of success. Anyhow, we shall have no delay or neglect now, but a wedding."

"Just gently," said the princess; "your wedding is not so short a way off as you suppose. Till I get the silver cup that my grandmother had at her wedding, and that my mother had as well, I will not marry, for I need to have it at my own wedding."

"You, rider of the black horse," said the Prince Underwaves, "I set you under spells and under crosses unless the silver cup is here before dawn to-morrow."

Out he went and reached the horse and leaned his elbow on his mane, and he heaved a sigh.

"Sigh of a king's son under spells!" said the horse; "mount and you shall get the silver cup. The people of the realm are gathered about the king to-night, for he has missed his daughter, and when you get to the palace go in and leave me without; they will have the cup there going round the company. Go in and sit in their midst. Say nothing, and seem to be as one of the people of the place. But when the cup comes round to you, take it under your oxter, and come out to me with it, and we'll go."

Away they went and they got to Greece, and he went in to the palace and did as the black horse bade. He took the cup and came out and mounted, and before sunrise he was in the Realm Underwaves.

"You are come," said Prince Underwaves.

"I am come," said he.

"We had better get married now," said the prince to the Greek princess.

"Slowly and softly," said she. "I will not marry till I get the silver ring that my grandmother and my mother wore when they were wedded."

"You, rider of the black horse," said the Prince Underwaves, "do that. Let's have that ring here to-morrow at sunrise."

The lad went to the black horse and put his elbow on his crest and told him how it was.

"There never was a matter set before me harder than this matter which has now been set in front of me," said the horse, "but there is no help for it at any rate. Mount me. There is a snow mountain and an ice mountain and a mountain of fire between us and the winning of that ring. It is right hard for us to pass them."

Thus they went as they were, and about a mile from the snow mountain they were in a bad case with cold. As they came near it he struck the horse, and with the bound he gave the black horse was on the top of the snow mountain; at the next bound he was on the top of the ice mountain; at the third bound he went through the mountain of fire. When he had passed the mountains he was dragging at the horse's neck, as though he were about to lose himself. He went on before him down to a town below.

"Go down," said the black horse, "to a smithy; make an iron spike for every bone end in me."

Down he went as the horse desired, and he got the spikes made, and back he came with them.

"Stick them into me," said the horse, "every spike of them in every bone end that I have."

That he did; he stuck the spikes into the horse.

"There is a loch here," said the horse, "four miles long and four miles wide, and when I go out into it the loch will take fire and blaze. If you see the Loch of Fire going out before the sun rises, expect me, and if not, go your way."

Out went the black horse into the lake, and the lake became flame. Long was he stretched about the lake, beating his palms and roaring. Day came, and the loch did not go out.

But at the hour when the sun was rising out of the water the lake went out.

And the black horse rose in the middle of the water with one single spike in him, and the ring upon its end.

He came on shore, and down he fell beside the loch.

Then down went the rider. He got the ring, and he dragged the horse down to the side of a hill. He fell to sheltering him with his arms about him, and as the sun was rising he got better and better, till about midday, when he rose on his feet.

"Mount," said the horse, "and let us be-gone."

He mounted on the black horse, and away they went.

He reached the mountains, and he leaped the horse at the fire mountain and was on the top. From the mountain of fire he leaped to the mountain of ice, and from the mountain of ice to the mountain of snow. He put the mountains past him, and by morning he was in the realm under the waves.

"You are come," said the prince.

"I am," said he.

"That's true," said Prince Underwaves. "A king's son are you, but a son of success am I. We shall have no more mistakes and delays, but a wedding this time."

"Go easy," said the Princess of the Greeks. "Your wedding is not so near as you think yet. Till you make a castle, I won't marry you. Not to your father's castle nor to your mother's will I go to dwell; but make me a castle for which your father's castle will not make washing water."

"You, rider of the black horse, make that," said Prince Underwaves, "before the morrow's sun rises."

The lad went out to the horse and leaned his elbow on his neck and sighed, thinking that this castle never could be made for ever.

"There never came a turn in my road yet that is easier for me to pass than this," said the black horse.

Glance that the lad gave from him he saw all that there were, and ever so many wrights and stone masons at work, and the castle was ready before the sun rose.

He shouted at the Prince Underwaves, and he saw the castle. He tried to pluck out his eye, thinking that it was a false sight.

"Son of King Underwaves," said the rider of the black horse, "don't think that you have a false sight; this is a true sight."

"That's true," said the prince. "You are a son of success, but I am a son of success too. There will be no more mistakes and delays, but a wedding now."

"No," said she. "The time is come. Should we not go to look at the castle? There's time enough to get married before the night comes."

They went to the castle and the castle was without a "but" ——

"I see one," said the prince. "One want at least to be made good. A well to be made inside, so that water may not be far to fetch when there is a feast or a wedding in the castle."

"That won't be long undone," said the rider of the black horse.

The well was made, and it was seven fathoms deep and two or three fathoms wide, and they looked at the well on the way to the wedding.

"It is very well made," said she, "but for one little fault yonder."

"Where is it?" said Prince Underwaves.

"There," said she.

He bent him down to look. She came out, and she put her two hands at his back, and cast him in.

"Be thou there," said she. "If I go to be married, thou art not the man; but the man who did each exploit that has been done, and, if he chooses, him will I have."

Away she went with the rider of the little black horse to the wedding.

And at the end of three years after that so it was that he first remembered the black horse or where he left him.

He got up and went out, and he was very sorry for his neglect of the black horse. He found him just where he left him.

"Good luck to you, gentleman," said the horse. "You seem as if you had got something that you like better than me."

"I have not got that, and I won't; but it came over me to forget you," said he.

"I don't mind," said the horse, "it will make no difference. Raise your sword and smite off my head."

"Fortune will now allow that I should do that," said he.

"Do it instantly, or I will do it to you," said the horse.

So the lad drew his sword and smote off the horse's head; then he lifted his two palms and uttered a doleful cry.

What should he hear behind him but "All hail, my brother-in-law."

He looked behind him, and there was the finest man he ever set eyes upon.

"What set you weeping for the black horse?" said he.

"This," said the lad, "that there never was born of man or beast a creature in this world that I was fonder of."

"Would you take me for him?" said the stranger.

"If I could think you the horse, I would; but if not, I would rather the horse," said the rider.

"I am the black horse," said the lad, "and if I were not, how should you have all these things that you went to seek in my father's house. Since I went under spells, many a man have I ran at before you met me. They had but one word amongst them: they could not keep me, nor manage me, and they never kept me a couple of days. But when I fell in with you, you kept me till the time ran out that was to come from the spells. And now you shall go home with me, and we will make a wedding in my father's house."

Seguing from fantasy to reality, I want to tell you about one of the greatest horses in history — if not *the* greatest. And certainly one of the most influential — if not *the* most influential. His name was Bucephalus, and he was the warhorse of Alexander the Great. His name in Greek, *Boukephalos,* means "Ox-head" — *bous* (meaning "ox") and *kephale* (meaning "head"). This had nothing to do with the horse being stubborn, though he may well have been; it refers to the bull's-head symbol which was either branded on his shoulder by Alexander or occurred there naturally. Sources I consulted say it was "imprinted," which could mean either. Still other sources maintain that the horse's head resembled that of a bull. It is not likely we will ever know for sure.

My career and the life of Alexander the Great are linked in the sense that I played him in a movie nearly a half a century ago. Obviously, that is very different from setting out to conquer the world. From this vantage point in my life, I can tell you that it's enough for a man to conquer himself, let alone everybody else. I didn't have that kind of stamina or vision in my youth. And even if I did have the vision, it's much different from the stamina those world-beaters had to have. But back to the boy-king.

Alexander was born in Pella, in the ancient kingdom of Macedon, in July of 356 BCE. A brilliant tactician, a great strategist, this young Macedonian king had conquered most of the known world by the time he was thirty. Think about that: he was a Millennial who ruled the world, though it was a much different millennium. He died two years later, of malaria, in what is now modern-day Iraq. I was several years older than that when I played him.

Here's the part about the stamina. Among his many achievements, Alexander was a renowned horseman. When he got this fractious black colt Bucephalus, nobody could train him. The so-called boy-king discovered what previous owners knew, that Bucephalus was afraid of his own shadow. That presented a challenge which Alexander embraced: he simply turned the horse in to the sun to train him so that the shadow did not exist. It is from that action, that act of turning him strategically in order to mount, that we get the phrase, "Having a leg up." Alexander also stopped wearing one of his favorite pieces of attire, a cloak, while he was training the horse, since that, too, alarmed Bucephalus.

Lest you think the shadow story is apocryphal, I've ridden horses that have tried to jump shadows on the ground because they weren't familiar with them. I make this point repeatedly throughout the book: horses can be bold and brave and they can also be skittish and craven. Some can endure cannon fire, others will flinch at a cracking branch. Part of what any rider has to do — and do well, if they want to continue to ride — is to understand this and be sensitive to the horse's own quirks and neuroses.

Bucephalus served Alexander well in combat after combat. By the time the charger perished, in 326 BCE — immediately after the Battle of the Hydaspes, which opened India to the Greeks — the legends of Alexander and Bucephalus were inseparable. So much so that every great commander thereafter, from Julius Caesar to Robert E. Lee, and every great cowboy, from Roy Rogers to the Lone Ranger, had to possess one great mount who was nearly as famed and beloved as the rider.

Mind you, Alexander was not infallible when it came to horses, and he appears to have been a bit of a know-it-all . . . until he wasn't. Initially, Alexander decried the invention of the saddle because he thought it was too sissified for his men. They all rode bareback, and powerfully so. When, some eight, nine years after he had begun his conquests — and toward the end of his incursion in the Mediterranean area — he came up to the Hindu Kush mountains in Central Asia, just short of invading India. There, he met and fought the tribesmen, who had saddles, and he had his first defeat as a general because the saddle gave the archers a more stable platform. A rider's purchase on the horse was increased enormously by the invention of the saddle. Alexander quickly and decisively changed his mind.

I do wonder what would have happened had the events been reversed and Alexander had predeceased Bucephalus. I suspect they would have been interred together. Or perhaps both would have ridden in one final battle, as the legendary "wonder horse" Babiéca did. He was the steed of Spain's great thirteenth-century national hero El Cid, "the Lord." Not only was Babiéca valiant in combat, but when El Cid died in battle the horse soldiered on, carrying his dead rider onward to the terror of the enemy, arrows reportedly striking the knight's bosom as he remained in his saddle.

Both of these examples are indicative of the horse-human relationship at its core, this idea of mutually beneficial codependence where each one uplifts the other to the next level — not just of mutual confidence but of leadership. This is a point that cannot be overstated.

Think of the great leaders — not just Alexander and El Cid but in modern times. The aforementioned Robert E. Lee, George S. Patton, George Washington, and Winston Churchill, all of them exceptional horsemen. These *leaders* (and I cannot emphasize that word enough) were able to encourage a horse to overcome their natural bent, which is to graze, to breed, and to die. Each of them was able to do the same thing with humans, to get panicking humans to override their own survival instincts and fight for the good of the whole.

What we see today are a lot of leaders who incite survival instincts rather than co-operation, with the result that people are becoming more aggressive and flighty rather than building or relying on the strength of the herd. We're losing that capacity of the individual to lead. We're losing that because people are not trained to ride anymore. We have people who have not served an apprenticeship commanding in the field, who have only sat at a desk all their lives, and as a result we're devolving. We're actually becoming more frightened and more aggressive, and inciting more fear and aggression in others, rather than overriding our basic survival instincts — which is the entire purpose of a "civilization," just as a herd: to provide mutual protection and empathy, to become elevated to a higher level of awareness and wisdom and what I would call evolution.

It's a disheartening state of affairs, especially to those of us who ride, who have seen how elevating these unions can be.

I had my Bucephalus. His name was Great Day and I'll tell you about him shortly. For now, though — a taste of Alexander and his great steed.

THE WAR HORSE OF ALEXANDER

BY ANDREW LANG,
FROM *The Animal Story Book* (1896)

Lang notes in his introduction to this tale that "part of the story of Bucephalus is taken from Plutarch," the famed Greek historian — as celebrated a narrative pedigree as one could hope for!

There are not so many stories about horses as there are about dogs and cats, yet almost every great general has had his favourite horse, who has gone with him through many campaigns and borne him safe in many battle-fields. At a town in Sicily called Agrigentum, they set such store by their horses, that pyramids were raised over their burial-place, and the Emperor Augustus built a splendid monument over the grave of an old favourite.

The most famous horse, perhaps, who ever lived, was one belonging to Alexander the Great, and was called Bucephalus. When the king was a boy, Bucephalus was brought before Philip, King of Macedon, Alexander's father, by Philonicus the Thessalian, and offered for sale for the large sum of thirteen talents. Beautiful though he was, Philip wisely declined to buy him before knowing what manner of horse he was, and ordered him to be led into a neighbouring field, and a groom to mount him. But it was in vain that the best and most experienced riders approached the horse; he reared up on his hind legs, and would suffer none to come near him. So Philonicus the Thessalian was told to take his horse back whence he came, for the king would have none of him.

Now the boy Alexander stood by, and his heart went out to the beautiful creature. And he cried out, "What a good horse do we lose for lack of skill to mount him!" Philip the king heard these words, and his soul was vexed to see the horse depart, but yet he knew not what else to do. Then he turned to Alexander and said: "Do you think that you, young and untried, can ride this horse better than those who have grown old in the stables?" To which Alexander made answer, "This horse I know I could ride better than they." "And if you fail," asked Philip, "what price will you pay for your good conceit of yourself?" And Alexander laughed out and said gaily, "I will pay the price of the horse." And thus it was settled.

So Alexander drew near to the horse, and took him by the bridle, turning his face to the sun so that he might not be frightened at the movements of his own shadow, for the prince had noticed that it scared him greatly. Then Alexander stroked his head and led him forwards, feeling his temper all the while, and when the horse began to get uneasy, the prince suddenly leapt on his back, and gradually curbed him with the bridle. Suddenly, as Bucephalus gave up trying to throw his rider, and only pawed the ground impatient to be off, Alexander shook the reins, and bidding him go, they flew like lightning round the course. This was Alexander's first conquest, and as he jumped down from the horse, his father exclaimed, "Go, my son, and seek for a kingdom that is worthy, for Macedon is too small for such as thee."

Henceforth Bucephalus made it clear that he served Alexander and no one else. He would submit quietly to having the gay trappings of a king's steed fastened on his head, and the royal saddle put on, but if any groom tried to mount him, back would go his ears and up would go his heels, and none dared come near him. For ten years after Alexander succeeded his father on the throne of Macedon (B.C. 336), Bucephalus bore him through all his battles, and was, says Pliny, "of a passing good and memorable service in the wars," and even when wounded, as he once was at the taking of Thebes, would not suffer his master to mount another horse. Together these two swam rivers, crossed mountains, penetrated into the dominions of the Great King, and farther still into the heart of Asia, beyond the Caspian and the river Oxus, where never a European army had gone before. Then turning sharp south, he crossed the range of the Hindoo Koosh, and entering the country of the Five Rivers, he prepared to attack Porus, king of India. But age and the wanderings of ten years had worn Bucephalus out. One last victory near the Hydaspes or Jelum, and the old horse sank down and died, full of years and honours (B.C. 326). Bitter were the lamentations of the king for the friend of his childhood, but his grief did not show itself only in weeping. The most splendid funeral Alexander could devise was given to Bucephalus, and a gorgeous tomb erected over his body. And more than that, Alexander resolved that the memory of his old horse should be kept green in these burning Indian deserts, thousands of miles from the Thessalian plains where he was born, so round his tomb the king built a city, and it was called:

"BUCEPHALIA."

OF WAR HORSES, OR DESTRIERS

Essays of Michel de Montaigne (1877)

This abridged essay provides a fascinating account of equestrian skills from around the world and from different times. It was written by a sixteenth-century philosopher-statesman, one of the greatest of his era.

I have read that the Romans had a sort of horses by them called "funales" or "dextrarios," which were either led horses, or horses laid on at several stages to be taken fresh upon occasion, and thence it is that we call our horses of service "destriers"; and our romances commonly use the phrase of "adestrer" for "accompagner," to accompany. They also called those that were trained in such sort, that running full speed, side by side, without bridle or saddle, the Roman gentlemen, armed at all pieces, would shift and throw themselves from one to the other, "desultorios equos." The Numidian men-at-arms had always a led horse in one hand, besides that they rode upon, to change in the heat of battle: "To whom it was a custom, leading along two horses, often in the hottest fight, to leap armed from a tired horse to a fresh one; so active were the men, and the horses so docile."

In the narrative which Philip de Commines has given of this battle, in which he himself was present, he tells us of wonderful performances by the horse on which the king was mounted. The name of the horse was Savoy, and it was the most beautiful horse he had ever seen. During the battle the king was personally attacked, when he had nobody near him but a valet de chambre, a little fellow, and not well armed. "The king," says Commines, "had the best horse under him in the world, and therefore he stood his ground bravely, till a number of his men, not a great way from him, arrived at the critical minute."

The Mamalukes make their boast that they have the most ready horses of any cavalry in the world; that by nature and custom they were taught to know and distinguish the enemy, and to fall foul upon them with mouth and heels, according to a word or sign given; as also to gather up with their teeth darts and lances scattered upon the field, and present them to their riders, on the word of command. 'T is said, both of Caesar and Pompey, that amongst their other excellent qualities they were both very good horsemen, and particularly of Caesar, that in his youth, being mounted on the bare back, without saddle or bridle, he could make the horse run, stop, and turn, and perform all its airs, with his hands behind him. As nature designed to make of this person, and of Alexander, two miracles of military art, so one would say she had done her utmost to arm them after an extraordinary manner for every one knows that Alexander's horse, Bucephalus, had a head inclining to the shape of a bull; that he would suffer himself to be mounted and governed by none but his master, and that he was so honoured after his death as to have a city erected to his name. Caesar had also one which had forefeet like those of a man, his hoofs being divided in the form of fingers, which likewise was not to be ridden, by any but Caesar himself, who, after his death, dedicated his statue to the goddess Venus.

I do not willingly alight when I am once on horseback, for it is the place where, whether well or sick, I find myself most at ease. Plato recommends it for health, as also Pliny says it is good for the stomach and the joints. Let us go further into this matter since here we are.

Our ancestors, and especially at the time

they had war with the English, in all their greatest engagements and pitched battles fought for the most part on foot, that they might have nothing but their own force, courage, and constancy to trust to in a quarrel of so great concern as life and honour. You stake your valour and your fortune upon that of your horse; his wounds or death bring your person into the same danger; his fear or fury shall make you reputed rash or cowardly; if he have an ill mouth or will not answer to the spur, your honour must answer for it. And, therefore, I do not think it strange that those battles were more firm and furious than those that are fought on horseback.

Caesar, speaking of the Suabians: "in the charges they make on horseback," says he, "they often throw themselves off to fight on foot, having taught their horses not to stir in the meantime from the place, to which they presently run again upon occasion; and according to their custom, nothing is so unmanly and so base as to use saddles or pads, and they despise such as make use of those conveniences: insomuch that, being but a very few in number, they fear not to attack a great many." That which I have formerly wondered at, to see a horse made to perform all his airs with a switch only and the reins upon his neck, was common with the Massilians, who rid their horses without saddle or bridle.

Xenophon tells us, that the Assyrians were fain to keep their horses fettered in the stable, they were so fierce and vicious; and that it required so much time to loose and harness them, that to avoid any disorder this tedious preparation might bring upon them in case of surprise, they never sat down in their camp till it was first well fortified with ditches and ramparts.

These new-discovered people of the Indies when the Spaniards first landed amongst them, had so great an opinion both of the men and horses, that they looked upon the first as gods and the other as animals ennobled above their nature; insomuch that after they were subdued, coming to the men to sue for peace and pardon, and to bring them gold and provisions, they failed not to offer of the same to the horses, with the same kind of harangue to them they had made to the others: interpreting their neighing for a language of truce and friendship.

I have seen a man ride with both his feet upon the saddle, take off his saddle, and at his return take it up again and replace it, riding all the while full speed; having galloped over a cap, make at it very good shots backwards with his bow; take up anything from the ground, setting one foot on the ground and the other in the stirrup: with twenty other ape's tricks, which he got his living by.

There has been seen in my time at Constantinople two men upon one horse, who, in the height of its speed, would throw themselves off and into the saddle again by turn; and one who bridled and saddled his horse with nothing but his teeth; another who betwixt two horses, one foot upon one saddle and the other upon another, carrying the other man upon his shoulders, would ride full career, the other standing bolt upright upon and making very good shots with his bow; several who would ride full speed with their heels upward, and their heads upon the saddle betwixt several scimitars, with the points upwards, fixed in the harness. When I was a boy, the prince of Sulmona, riding an unbroken horse at Naples, prone to all sorts of action, held reals [*small coins*] under his knees and toes, as if they had been nailed there, to shew the firmness of his seat.

WILD HORSES

As the saga of Bucephalus indicates, wild horses are elemental. Each one is as big as all outdoors, fickle as a knee-high dust devil. Together, in a herd, they are so much more. In mathematics, you would say that the whole is greater than the sum of the parts. This is particularly true of herds, and it is even more particularly true of American herds. I put it to you that the idea of "American exceptionalism" began with the horse.

Consider this: they were transported to these shores in a totally foreign way, on ancient, leaky boats. Those that had shied forcefully from the plank on other shores were probably not forced to board. They never would have survived. What about those who did? What do you think the impact was on the horses who got off of those boats? Only the best endured, brought here by the Spaniards to Central America and the English to the colonies. Those two groups of exceptional horses, some of them becoming free and wild, met somewhere in the center of the country and formed bands of wild horses, mustangs, and these were the best mating with the best. One can well imagine the Quarter Horse deriving its strength and its courage and its popularity in America from that singular fact.

When I was a boy — and even now, as a much older boy — one of the most thrilling images I saw in films or storybooks or in my mind's eye was a herd of wild horses roaming free. Whether they were in a relaxed state, grazing in majestic repose, or in a riot of movement, wild horses were a special sight, a special concept. When we think of elemental forces like fires or storms or earthquakes, human beings are at their mercy. We fight them or survive them, we do not hope to tame them. A herd of horses is at the outer limits of what can, in theory, be controlled. And, controlling them, humans can outrace winds and floods and flame.

Even with my untrained eye those many years ago, I was sure I could pick out the leader of the herd in a film. Now, of course, I know I can. He's usually a stallion, very strong, very sensitive. As in a deer herd or other male-dominated groups of animals, he is absolutely alert to any change in his environment. He races up and down, guiding the herd, being responsible for so many things: for breeding the mares, for collecting strays, for driving off other stallions or predators.

To put it bluntly, a leader watches after the herd and also protects his own ass.

Eventually, after a leader has accumulated a lot of mileage, a younger horse will challenge him and inevitably take over after a spirited fight. The leader is smart. He knows what's coming. He's watched as the young animals — his own sons — get larger and larger, faster and faster. Often, the leader may kick that young stallion out, thereby alleviating the interbreeding that could occur. But eventually those two-year-old, or yearling, male horses turn three and four, come to the fullness of their strength, and come back to fight their father.

In our society, that kind of conflict is the stuff of Shakespearean drama. Except for the fact that horses are vegetarians, James Goldman's magnificent play *The Lion in Winter,* about Henry II fighting off his patricidal-fratricidal sons, could have been *The Horse in Winter.* Maintaining leadership of a herd is bare-hooves brawling!

There is a great lesson in this process, however. Unlike in the world of predators — and I include humans in this — the horse that has lost is not pursued by the victor. As soon as one animal adjourns the competition, the other moves off. In the society of horses, there is something ancient and poignant about what follows. Especially when we consider that while the king of the hill may be ousted, effectively discarded, the wise old mare of the herd is respected and is very much a dominant force. This is in keeping with the ways of many other animals, such as elephants and lions, where the society is fundamentally matriarchal.

The end of any life spent in charge of anything is always a time for reflection, and I imagine that in his own way the deposed herd leader — if he hasn't been seriously injured — reflects on the past in some fundamental way. Perhaps he visualizes or smells or hears echoes. Perhaps it's less fleeting and specific than that, maybe it's the same things that appealed to me as a boy, to so many of us: the vanished "days of yesteryear" when there was nothing but the promise of the future and the wonder of the open plains.

But you see, in this innate sense of freedom, the difficulty any trainer faces in order to train them. You're bringing to bear things like the lead line, the lash whip, the saddle, the blanket, the bridle . . . you're presenting a lot of new things that horses intuitively choose to flee from, rather than subject themselves to. How do you overcome that?

Stacy Westfall, a wonderful trainer, has a unique approach. She believes, and I agree, that horses can read intentions really well. Prey animals must do that: think of a deer, always alert. And when you approach them, your intention — whether it is to conquer them, whether it is to see this process from their point of view — is quickly apparent to the horse. Even your body or something you're innocently carrying with you — like my hat — can be terrifying. So you have to begin by understanding that the horse needs to have choices. Think of any human situation. When we think about a boss who is effective, they could be effective as a leader, or they could be effective as a dictator, and each creates a different feeling in the office. If a trainer senses they are experiencing apprehension, you have to work around it with them, instead of just forcing them. For example, if you are working inside a round pen, you give them the choice of staying and perhaps being rubbed with a blanket, or leaving. It requires a lot of patience and empathy. Forcing them, I believe, is a mistake. You can certainly make a horse stand still, but the horse will always be scared. It would be similar to saying, "Oh, you're scared of spiders? Let me tie you to this chair near a spider and then you'll get over it."

Stacy, for one, doesn't even train a horse with reins or a saddle. She rides bareback, which is as close to the horse being in the wild, with freedom of choice, as it can be. You make the horse a partner rather than an employee. The value of this process is that it's a lot like recognizing talent in children. You may make them take piano lessons or play baseball, but what if their talent is drawing? Or running? If you work with a child or a horse, let their own inter-est and talent lead them, as they move through the process they — and you — will discover where their greatest strength lies.

In a way, that's how a herd operates: it's a form of natural selection. And through this process the trainer joins body and spirit with the horse so that both are enhanced. You know when that occurs: it happens in little moments, micro-moments that string together and suddenly, like falling in love, everything is *different*.

Believe it or not, the horse understands

this. Because, in effect, you are becoming a herd of two.

This leads to the question of whether a human can be even more than that: a member of the herd, the way Dian Fossey lived among mountain gorillas in Rwanda. There is significant evidence that horses reach out to us as much as or more than we reach out to them, and it is not impossible to say where this will lead: a true pan-species unity, where the most empathic among both are one!

It's conceivable. I heard a story about just such a partnership, told by naturalist Joe Hutto, a gentleman who lived on a farm in the wilds of Montana. He became acquainted with a herd of mule deer, got to know individuals — in particular the occasional diplomat who would come and visit with him . . . then all of them would visit with him. And over a period of five, six years, he actually became part of the herd. They would groom each other, and he was able to saunter out into the wilds with them. In fauning, when they would bear the young in the spring, the mule deer brought these young to him and somehow communicated to the fauns that he was not a danger, was part of the herd. Yet they were always on guard for any stranger that might come over. They'd run away from anybody else, but not him.

There *are* exceptional beings like this in any herd, probably more than we know, that through a mixture of courage and curiosity have brought their fellows to different places in their environment, including making friends with human beings. How many undocumented instances are there, I wonder, from the seventeenth and eighteenth centuries, and among Native Americans?

Which brings up the question of horse intelligence. There was a trainer I met, a woman, who had this particularly alert horse, and the horse would let everyone know when she arrived at the stables. It would start becoming agitated.

So one day the trainer said, "I'm going to fool the horse. I'm not going to come in at the regular time, and I'll come in silently."

It didn't matter. Everything she did, no matter how quietly, how silently — there was nothing she could do that would change the ability of the horse to recognize her. I've also heard of this with dogs.

So these animals are smart. But what if they became even smarter . . . ?

GULLIVER'S TRAVELS

BY JONATHAN SWIFT (1726)

The herd is a wondrous thing because whatever intelligence guides it is fundamentally pure instinct, evolved and sharpened and elevated over millennia.

What would happen if that development were to continue? Or what if the roles were reversed, if it were the humans who were wild and the horses who were civilized?

Author Pierre Boulle imagined something like that in his classic 1963 novel *Planet of the Apes,* which became the basis for the science-fiction film franchise — and in which, you may recall, horses play a vital part, serving the intelligent apes in the same way they serve intelligent humans.

But centuries before the French author wrote his novel, Jonathan Swift used a similar idea involving horses.

You probably remember the most famous fictional voyages of Dr. Lemuel Gulliver, a ship's surgeon, who set sail in 1699 and was the sole survivor of a shipwreck, which deposited him in Lilliput, a land of very tiny people; leaving there, he ended up in Brobdingnag, a land of giants.

But Gulliver had many other adventures, the last of which (excerpted here) was in the land of the Houyhnhnms, a civilization where the humans were beasts known as Yahoos, and the horses were the thoughtful, educated, articulate masters.

Swift was a cynic, certainly a curmudgeon. Those qualities inhabit virtually every paragraph. (Don't take just my word for it. This is the author who gave us "A Modest Proposal," an essay which suggests a solution to famine and overpopulation in one, grim swoop.)

By the way, the tongue-tripping name for the horses was apparently pronounced "Hwinnem," since the author meant for all Houyhnhnm words to sound like neighing.

Herewith are sections of Gulliver's lengthy visit, beginning with the first meeting between educated man and educated horse . . . and concluding with the horse's very logical reason for disbelieving what he's been told!

I saw a horse walking softly in the field; which my persecutors having sooner discovered, was the cause of their flight. The horse started a little, when he came near me, but soon recovering himself, looked full in my face with manifest tokens of wonder; he viewed my hands and feet, walking round me several times. I would have pursued my journey, but he placed himself directly in the way, yet looking with a very mild aspect, never offering the least violence. We stood gazing at each other for some time; at last I took the boldness to reach my hand towards his neck with a design to stroke it, using the common style and whistle of jockeys, when they are going to handle a strange horse. But this animal seemed to receive my civilities with disdain, shook his head, and bent his brows, softly raising up his right forefoot to remove my hand. Then he neighed three or four times, but in so different a cadence, that I almost began to think he was speaking to himself, in some language of his own.

While he and I were thus employed, another horse came up; who applying himself to the first in a very formal manner, they gently struck each other's right hoof before, neighing several times by turns, and varying the sound, which seemed to be almost articulate. They went some paces off, as if it were to confer together, walking side by side, backward and forward, like persons deliberating upon some affair of weight, but often turning their eyes towards me, as it were to watch that I might not escape. I was amazed to see such actions and behaviour in brute beasts; and concluded with myself, that if the inhabitants of this country were endued with a proportionable degree of reason, they must needs be the wisest people upon earth. This thought gave me so much comfort, that I resolved to go forward, until I could discover some house or village, or meet with any of the natives, leaving the two horses to discourse together as they pleased. But the first, who was a dapple gray, observing me to steal off, neighed after me in so expressive a tone, that I fancied myself to understand what he meant; whereupon I turned back, and came near to him to expect his farther commands: but concealing my fear as much as I could, for I began to be in some pain how this adventure might terminate; and the reader will easily believe I did not much like my present situation.

The two horses came up close to me, looking with great earnestness upon my face and hands. The gray steed rubbed my hat all round with his right fore-hoof, and discomposed it so much that I was forced to adjust it better by taking it off and settling it again; whereat, both he and his companion (who was a brown bay) appeared to be much surprised: the latter felt the lappet of my coat, and finding it to hang loose about me, they both looked with new signs of wonder.

He stroked my right hand, seeming to admire the softness and colour; but he squeezed it so hard between his hoof and his pastern, that I was forced to roar; after which they both touched me with all possible tenderness. They were under great perplexity about my shoes and stockings, which they felt very often, neighing to each other, and using various gestures, not unlike those of a philosopher, when he would attempt to solve some new and difficult phenomenon.

I could frequently distinguish the word Yahoo, which was repeated by each of them several times: and although it was impossible for me to conjecture what it meant, yet while the two horses were busy in conversation, I endeavoured to practise this word upon my tongue; and as soon as they were silent, I boldly pronounced Yahoo in a loud voice, imitating at the same time, as near as I could, the neighing of a horse; at which they were both visibly surprised; and the gray repeated the same word twice, as if he meant to teach me the right accent; wherein I spoke after him as well as I could, and found myself perceivably to improve every time, though very far from any degree of perfection. Then the bay tried me with a second word, much harder to be pronounced; but reducing it to the English orthography, may be spelt thus, Houyhnhnm. I did not succeed in this so well as in the former; but after two or three farther trials, I had better fortune; and they both appeared amazed at my capacity.

He afterwards showed me a wisp of hay, and a fetlock full of oats; but I shook my head, to signify that neither of these were food for me.

He then put his fore-hoof to his mouth, at which I was much surprised, although he did it with ease, and with a motion that appeared perfectly natural, and made other signs, to know what I would eat; but I could not return him such an answer as he was able to apprehend; and if he had understood me, I did not see how it was possible to contrive any way for finding myself nourishment. While we were thus engaged, I observed a cow passing by, whereupon I pointed to her, and expressed a desire to go and milk her. This had its effect; for he led me back into the house, and ordered a mare-servant to open a room, where a good store of milk lay in earthen and wooden vessels, after a very orderly and cleanly manner. She gave me a large bowlful, of which I drank very heartily, and found myself well refreshed.

My principal endeavour was to learn the language, which my master (for so I shall henceforth call him), and his children, and every servant of his house, were desirous to teach me; for they looked upon it as a prodigy, that a brute animal should discover such marks of a rational creature. I pointed to every thing, and inquired the name of it, which I wrote down in my journal-book when I was alone, and corrected my bad accent by desiring those of the family to pronounce it often. In this employment, a sorrel nag, one of the under-servants, was very ready to assist me.

The word Houyhnhnm, in their tongue, signifies a horse, and, in its etymology, the perfection of nature. I told my master that "I was at a loss for expression, but would improve as fast as I could; and hoped, in a short time, I should be able to tell him wonders." He was pleased to direct his own mare, his colt, and foal, and the servants of the family, to take all opportunities of instructing me; and every day, for two or three hours, he was at the same pains himself. Several horses and mares of quality in the neighbourhood came often to our house, upon the report spread of "a wonderful Yahoo, that could speak like a Houyhnhnm, and seemed, in his words and actions, to discover some glimmerings of reason." These delighted to converse with me: they put many questions, and received such answers as I was able to return. By all these advantages I made so great a progress, that, in five months from my arrival I understood whatever was spoken, and could express myself tolerably well.

When I asserted that the Yahoos were the only governing animals in my country, which my master said was altogether past his conception, he desired to know, "whether we had Houyhnhnms among us, and what was their employment?" I told him, "we had great numbers; that in summer they grazed in the fields, and in winter were kept in houses with hay and oats, where Yahoo servants were employed to rub their skins smooth, comb their manes, pick their feet, serve them with food, and make their beds." "I understand you well," said my master: "it is now very plain, from all you have spoken, that whatever share of reason the Yahoos pretend to, the Houyhnhnms are your masters; I heartily wish our Yahoos would be so tractable." I begged "his honour would please to excuse me from proceeding any further, because I was very certain that the account he expected from me would be highly displeasing." But he insisted in commanding me to let him know the best and the worst.

I told him "he should be obeyed." I owned that "the Houyhnhnms among us, whom we called horses, were the most generous and comely animals we had; that they excelled in strength and swiftness; and when they belonged to persons of quality, were employed in travelling, racing, or drawing chariots; they were treated with much kindness and care, till they fell into diseases, or became foundered in the feet; but then they were sold, and used to all kind of drudgery till they died; after which their skins were stripped, and sold for what they were worth, and their bodies left to be devoured by dogs and birds of prey. But the common race of horses had not so good fortune, being kept by farmers and carriers, and other mean people, who put them to greater labour, and fed them worse." I described, as well as I could, our way of riding; the shape and use of a bridle, a saddle, a spur, and a whip; of harness and wheels. I added, "that we fastened plates of a certain hard substance, called iron, at the bottom of their feet, to preserve their hoofs from being broken by the stony ways, on which we often travelled."

My master, after some expressions of great indignation, wondered "how we dared to venture upon a Houyhnhnm's back; for he was sure, that the weakest servant in his house would be able to shake off the strongest Yahoo; or by lying down and rolling on his back, squeeze the brute to death."

HORSING AROUND ON THE SET

I have to tell you a story that has very little to do with horses, but has more to do with something one horse brought into my life. It's among my most treasured memories from shooting any film or TV episode with a Western theme. We were filming an episode of *Star Trek,* one that involved horses. Actually, it involved *a* horse, and also a tiger. Strangely, the episode was not the third-season "Spectre of the Gun," our only Western, which had no horses. In "Spectre," crew members had been captured by an alien whose idea of fun was to drop us into a re-creation of the gunfight at the O.K. Corral. It was shot entirely on soundstages and was a bit of déjà vu for DeForest Kelley because a dozen years before he had costarred as Morgan Earp alongside Burt Lancaster and Kirk Douglas in the film *Gunfight at the O.K. Corral.* (I suppose it would have been doubly fitting if "Dr. Mc-

Coy" had played Doc Holliday instead of Kirk, but I digress. . . .)

The episode in question was from the first season and it was called "Shore Leave." We shot on location at the famed Vasquez Rocks in Agua Dulce, California, with Leonard Nimoy, myself, and DeForest. One scene called for a knight on horseback to run a lance through DeForest, and another involved a tiger who was discreetly chained to the ground a few yards away.

The great thing about locations, even for TV, is that you often go to some mountain or valley or ranch or forest well outside the city. You always have to get up real early in the morning, because first you have to get there, and then you have to go to makeup. After that, if a horse is involved, there's also the matter of getting the horse calmed and familiar with the location and ready to shoot.

While that's going on, you have time to sit. Leonard and I were already in our Starfleet wardrobe. We had gone to the food-services truck to get something suitably rustic — an egg sandwich with onions on toasted rye bread and coffee — and then we sat there, not far from where the one horse was kept, watching the sun rise. This particular day, the sun set the sky aflame as it rose, and it was like a dream — it struck us both the same way. The dream was the skies coming to life, the privilege of doing what we were doing — it was a memory we both cherished.

Now, I love the other kinds of location moments too. You know, driving a fast car and skidding ninety feet to a stop on a cliff like we were on — which I have also done. But standing near a settled horse, with no pressure to do anything other than absorb the morning and eat the sandwich, that was magic.

The irony, of course, is that I'm a Canadian Jew, Leonard was a Boston Jew, and we were eating something classically New York. But somehow it said "daylight and open spaces" and it was delightful, just us with the strong smell of onions and the animal now waiting patiently nearby.

Obviously, the tiger was not present *that* day: otherwise, the horse would never have calmed. Interestingly, when the caged cat did arrive, there was nothing restful about the location. It was electric with his ferocity.

On Westerns, or on any film with horses, things are not usually that placid.

What horses do, most immediately, is bring you humility. Whenever you think you're doing something well on a horse, whenever you think, "Oh, I am really good," the horse immediately, within a short while, shows you the wrongness of your conclusion. That is a lesson I remember every time I am on horseback. *Every* time.

Before I did *Star Trek,* there was a Western episode that I made for television — it may have been on *Outlaws* or *The Big Valley,* I did a lot of those shows — where the horse had to fall in front of the camera. They were going to do it the usual way, with a stunt guy looking something like me, galloping toward the camera and falling to the ground. Then they'd cut, bring the camera in, and I'd be the one to get up off the ground. That was how those things were done to prevent injury to the actor.

Being young and adventurous — or foolhardy, or maybe all three — I said, "I can do this, and make it one continuous take."

No one raised any objections. They must have thought I knew what I was doing.

It was the evening, and they dug up the earth to make it softer, and they wet the ground down because it looks better wet — it photographs more like earth — and then there were some delays. And that's important because when I went to do the stunt, the ground was not damp but muddy. So I rode toward the camera, pulled the horse's head around in a flying W— a way of bringing the horse down without injury to the horse — it fell exactly as it was supposed to . . . and I didn't get out of the way because a) the wet ground had turned muddy and was like clay; and b) my left leg ended up under the horse. The horse couldn't get up, and it was struggling to get up. I was pinned there and struggling to get up. Even then, I was still okay. Until the horse finally *did* manage to get up and stepped on my leg, breaking it. Keep in mind, the cameras were still rolling.

I wanted to finish this shot so badly that when the horse got up and got away from the frame of the camera, and the director still hadn't called cut, I rose painfully and stood there doing my dialogue, and I'm shaking with shock. Judging from the faces of the crew, everyone, including the director, thought I was giving the performance of a lifetime. In a way, I was. Method acting at its best. But as soon as the shock was over, I fell back into the mud and didn't get up. They took me to Los Angeles County Hospital, downtown Los Angeles, to put me in a cast.

The strange or wonderful thing is, even when I was waiting in the hospital for medical care, my leg numb, I was very much aware of these amazing people working around me, as gunshot victims from gang warfare in downtown L.A. came in and out. Finally, I saw an emergency doctor; he looked like God, coming over in all his whites, handsome guy, and I thought, "Good Lord, this guy is exactly who you want to see when you come into an emergency hospital." Yet at that same moment, lying there on the gurney, I also saw the black shoes and white socks of the policemen who were handcuffed to gunshot thugs of all stripes. I always try to look at the positives of any experience, and seeing a county hospital from the point of view of a patient was certainly that.

Getting back to the stunt, it was quite an experience to do it, have it on camera, be in such extreme pain as a broken leg, and it ending with me in a cast for a couple of weeks, not riding a horse for the rest of that episode and only doing close-ups. At the time, though, I looked at the mishap as a freak event. I know better now.

Another rewarding piece I did on horseback was the TV miniseries *The Bastard,* in 1978, based on the big bestseller about the Revolutionary War. I got to play one of the most famous riders this side of Lady Godiva: Paul Revere. By that time I was a pretty decent horseman and made a convincing show of riding forth to "give the alarm."

Beyond a doubt, though, the two films I did on horseback that were most memorable to me were one I mentioned earlier, the TV movie *Alexander the Great,* and the feature film *White Comanche,* which I shot in Spain. The first one I made in 1964 as a TV pilot — quite an elaborate and expensive one, for its day. The latter was shot in 1968, when *Star Trek* was on hiatus.

Alexander the Great had a terrific cast. Costarring was another actor soon to take TV by storm: Adam West, TV's Batman. Alexander, of course, was a dream part and it was a very vital, energetic production, much of it shot on locations in Southern California — locations that passed well enough for the ancient times and the sandy, sun-bedazzled hills and plains where they were taking place. I did a lot of riding in that one: rearing on a beach, galloping across a field, fighting with enemies — I loved every minute of it. I had already discovered that I was a good natural horseman, if not the world's most adept stuntman; I was at least good enough to convince myself and the director I could do most of the action scenes. I wasn't, not really, but

I'll get to that in a bit.

Let me state the obvious: basic horseman-ship skills are important if you're going to convince an audience that you are the person you're playing in a Western or historical film. I'm not just talking about riding, I mean just sitting there in front of the camera. The horse isn't in on the agenda. It wants to eat, sleep, have sex, or leave in search of one of the above. You've got to be able to control the animal at least that much.

For this shoot I was able to do that, and also control the horse for close-ups and the run-bys — which is when you turn away in a long shot and run by the camera. *Most* actors can sit on a horse in close-up, and when they start to wheel the horse away from the camera there's an immediate cut and then a stuntman gets on that horse, or a similar horse, and rides off at a gallop so the actor is not in jeopardy on rough ter-rain.

You will also notice, watching films with horses, that built in to many scenes — this was certainly true in *Alexander the Great* — one of the other riders or some other character will come over and hold the bridle while the mounted rider is delivering lines. That's to let the actor concentrate on dialogue without worrying that the horse is suddenly going to take a little walk. Or else you can be assured that there are one or more persons holding on to the horse off-camera, because the horse does get restless after a while and then there is always the chance, on location, that something could spook them, be it a bird or a crew member or the wind causing your cloak to flutter.

A bit of a digression, here. During the heyday of the Hollywood Westerns, in the 1930s, 1940s, and 1950s — which is when the genre shifted to TV — the San Fernando Valley was awash with horses trained to do Westerns. These animals knew how to stand very still while the camera was rolling and remained relatively calm around guns firing blanks and people yelling and screaming. (You don't want them *too* calm or the scene will be unrealistic: a Civil War battle with horses grazing?) These horses also had to come when a rider like Gene Autry or Jimmy Wakely whistled for them, which horses do not do in real life. Before the ASPCA rightly became involved, the horse was propelled toward the whistler by a BB gun pellet fired into its rump.

That pool of horse talent had dwindled by the time I did *Alexander the Great,* though for all the action it was a very smooth shoot.

Thinking back, I wonder if my conviction that I was Alexander and this horse *was* Bucephalus was somehow communicated to the animal. I like to believe it was.

My other project that year, *White Comanche,* was a little rockier. This one was a theatrical film shot in Spain and I played two roles: cowboy Johnny Moon and his slightly unhinged bare-chested Native American twin brother, Notah. We eventually have a *High Noon* showdown in town . . . charging one another on horseback and drawing at full gallop. I won.

Now, this shoot was even further along in that period I was just discussing, when Hollywood had stopped making traditional Westerns. By 1969 they were hardly making any kind of Westerns at all. This was the era of the antiheroic films like *Easy Rider* — but in Spain and Italy, the so-called spaghetti Westerns were suddenly very popular. That's why Clint Eastwood went there, Eli Wallach, Lee Van Cleef, and many others who had worked in the Western genre. The demand for Hollywood actors who had international recognition was great.

So off I went, too. It may not have been a brilliant project but sometimes actors do things because they get to spend time in another country. I know that's why some

Hollywood actors went to Japan around this time to shoot Godzilla movies, of all things; they got paid to work in Tokyo.

That entire film was fun. I had two horses, though not for the reasons you might expect; they weren't for the brothers but to perform different functions on-screen. This is not uncommon. Charlton Heston had two identical stallions for his 1961 epic *El Cid,* one for moving easily among other horses and actors, the other for charging sure-footed on the beach and icy mountain passes. (Heston once remarked, "You haven't lived until you've jumped on a saddle, in stiff chain mail, at five in the morning on a frozen hilltop.") In fact, Chuck used to tell a story about the wrangler bringing the wrong horse for the scene in which El Cid was supposed to be propped, dead, in the saddle to lead the climactic charge. If you watch the film you can see that this horse just wanted to run, not parade to the battlefield. It turns one way, then another, and you can also see Chuck heroically preventing it from doing so with just his legs . . . since he was supposed to be dead. It's a masterful job, one that most viewers probably wouldn't notice. Which is the point.

White Comanche was shot, fittingly, at the

soundstages and back lot of the former Bronston Productions, where *El Cid* had been made. Like Heston, I had a horse they named El Nervioso as the long-distance horse, the horse I would ride at a gallop, and then they had the close-up horse, El Tranquilo, who would be calm when the clapboard clacked in his face and I had to wheel the horse away and ride off into the sunset.

As it turned out, before too long the horses had to trade roles, because after my guidance and ability to control him, El Nervioso gradually calmed down, became very tranquil. Meanwhile, El Tranquilo was getting real nervous about people jumping up and down in front of the camera, and he became El Nervioso. So then we had to switch the horses.

Of all of the horse stuff that I did over my career, that was the most challenging and also the most fun. I enjoyed "reading" the horses, if you will, knowing just when it was time to swap one for the other.

This would probably be a good time to mention another challenge on the shoot: I rode these two horses bareback, which added to the danger. I learned to do this under the aegis of Glenn Randall, Jr., one of those gentlemen who, like Yakima Canutt (more on *that* legend later), was born to do what he did. His father had been a renowned rodeo rider and movie horseman before him. Glenn Jr. went on to become a masterly stunt coordinator for films that didn't have any horses, like *The Towering Inferno* and *E.T.,* but back then he was still in the original family business of horses.

With Glenn's help I became competent enough but, obviously, as I said, riding bareback adds another level of danger to anything beyond a trot. And it was very stupid of me to ride El Nervioso that way, across a field, because with some frequency horses break their legs stepping in a gopher hole. And everybody knew that, including me. I had the arrogance going in — but as the days passed, and I became aware of just how many things could have gone wrong, I was forced to reevaluate my skill level. I was also a little more mindful of the risks than I'd been in other films. As on the plains of the American West, there are many potential life-ending scenarios that come from riding a horse full-out on a prairie. I would take time to walk whatever path I was supposed to follow, looking for pitfalls.

Glenn also showed me how to do a stunt that I really loved. It was a trick of rolling backward off the horse as the horse was cantering along, as if I'd been shot. The idea was I'd fall backward, land on my feet, and then fall on the ground — secretly fine, thus luring the enemy in. I pulled it off, though I can only imagine what these Spanish guys who knew and loved horses really thought of me, so eager and cocksure. But then, as I said about *Alexander the Great,* I didn't want a stuntman having to double for me in a single scene. I wanted to do it all. And that's what I did.

Thanks to Glenn and whatever guardian angel was watching over me, nothing happened, I never got hurt on that shoot, but as I look back on it now I think, "How could you have done that?"

There is one more story I'd like to share, one that has nothing to do with riding but with the larger theme of this book, the spiritual magic of the horse.

In 2002, I was directing a movie called *Groom Lake,* about a woman's search for extraterrestrial life. We were shooting in Arizona, right near the border between Mexico and Arizona. When we were shooting at night, every so often the lights would pick up some individuals coming over a rise. And we were told that it was dangerous because that location was near a known border crossing. The "coyotes," the leaders

133

of the border crossers, were taking people across in groups and it could be risky for us since we were there with cameras possibly photographing people who absolutely did not want to be discovered.

In addition, not because we were there, but as a matter of course, border guards would often turn up, walking in the dark, and would come into the frame, and we would have to stop shooting. You wouldn't think shooting on location, in your own land, could be so difficult and treacherous, but there you are.

Eventually I made friends with some of the border guards, and they invited me to come and patrol the border. That's the kind of experience you don't pass up, and when I wasn't shooting at night, and my preparations for the next day were done, I went with them. My wife Elizabeth was with me.

She and I got into a car and drove to the border to meet these two border guards, and one of them said, "We know both of you are interested in horses, and we have horses here that we took from the 'coyotes.' " So Elizabeth and I got on the two horses and the border guards were on foot; Elizabeth is an expert rider, having trained horses for most of her life. They handed us night-vision goggles so that we could see — albeit in that eerie, luminous shade of green — and we went into the brush, which had a great deal of cactus. The border guards knew the cactus, the horses knew the cactus because they were desert horses, and we got to that rise where we'd been seeing people all through the shoot. It was a swell in the earth, and the border guards whispered, "The border is right over there, let's stay here for a moment."

We all stood silently under the night sky, practically no light at all, just starlight. And the horses too stood, immobile.

And I whispered, "What exactly are we waiting for?"

And the border guard said, "These horses were mistreated by the guys running the people. They hated the people that owned them. When we confiscated these animals, we realized that their ears would move, that they would look in the direction that the 'coyotes' were coming, were bringing people across the border, because they were so apprehensive about their former owners that they would immediately be alerted. And only they could hear and smell what the human beings, the rest of us, could not."

So now we're in that situation, and suddenly both horses swivel and point in the same direction. And the guards start running off into the dark, and we're on the horses and we're riding to keep up — because we did not want to be there unprotected. We're racing past cactus, over brush, and we can't even see who we're pursuing — even though we can "see" in the dark! And suddenly we come upon a group of twenty-five people huddled, getting ready to be moved on into the United States. The guards said, "Now you all sit there and put your hands above your head." And they arrested the guide. The horses did not relax, but we comforted them, assured them that all was well. The sensitivity of these horses was both impressive . . . and very, very moving.

But there's a coda.

As Elizabeth and I are sitting on these horses, looking at these poor people who are trying to come to America, we've got the night goggles on and now I can see this one particular guy, a young Mexican fellow, and he looks up at me and he says with a curious sense of awe and disbelief: "Captain Kirk."

THE HORSEMAN IN THE SKY

BY AMBROSE BIERCE (1889)

A number of years ago, I made two appearances on a television series called *The Twilight Zone.* It was a consistently ingenious, artful anthology series shepherded by the brilliant Rod Serling, and it featured tales of science fiction and fantasy. Throughout its five-year run — that number does seem to follow me around! — all of the stories were shot expressly for the show . . . save one. The exception was the chilling "An Occurrence at Owl Creek Bridge," a Civil War story written by Ambrose Bierce. It was filmed in Europe and won an Oscar for best live-action short subject. Rod Serling snapped it up to present on his series.

Bierce (1842–1914) was a soldier, author, critic, journalist, and all-around misanthrope (his nickname was "Bitter Bierce") whose works tended to be pessimistic at best, nightmarish at worst. He spent a lot of time on horseback in the rugged Dakota Territory, in Texas, and in revolutionary Mexico — where he vanished, his fate a mystery.

While this story is not about a horse per se, the mount is surely essential . . . and its role in the tale unique. And it could easily have been an episode of the aforementioned TV classic!

I

One sunny afternoon in the autumn of the year 1861 a soldier lay in a clump of laurel by the side of a road in western Virginia. He lay at full length upon his stomach, his feet resting upon the toes, his head upon the left forearm. His extended right hand loosely grasped his rifle. But for the somewhat methodical disposition of his limbs and a slight rhythmic movement of the cartridge-box at the back of his belt he might have been thought to be dead. He was asleep at his post of duty. But if detected he would be dead shortly afterward, death being the just and legal penalty of his crime.

The clump of laurel in which the criminal lay was in the angle of a road which after ascending southward a steep acclivity to that point turned sharply to the west, running along the summit for perhaps one hundred yards. There it turned southward again and went zigzagging downward through the forest. At the salient of that second angle was a large flat rock, jutting out northward, overlooking the deep valley from which the road ascended. The rock capped a high cliff; a stone dropped from its outer edge would have fallen sheer downward one thousand feet to the tops of the pines. The angle where the soldier lay was on another spur of the same cliff. Had he been awake he would have commanded a view, not only of the short arm of the road and the jutting rock, but of the entire profile of the cliff below it. It might well have made him giddy to look.

The country was wooded everywhere except at the bottom of the valley to the northward, where there was a small natural meadow, through which flowed a stream scarcely visible from the valley's rim. This open ground looked hardly larger than an ordinary door-yard, but was really several acres in extent. Its green was more vivid than that of the inclosing forest. Away beyond it rose a line of giant cliffs similar to those upon which we are supposed to stand in our survey of the savage scene, and through which the road had somehow made its climb to the summit. The configuration of the valley, indeed, was such that from this point of observation it seemed entirely shut in, and one could but have wondered how the road which found a way out of it had found a way into it, and whence came and whither went the waters of the stream that parted the meadow more than a thousand feet below.

No country is so wild and difficult but men will make it a theatre of war; concealed in the forest at the bottom of that military rat-trap, in which half a hundred men in possession of the exits might have starved an army to submission, lay five regiments of Federal infantry. They had marched all the previous day and night and were resting. At nightfall they would take to the road again, climb to the place where their unfaithful sentinel now slept, and descending the other slope of the ridge fall upon a camp of the enemy at about midnight. Their hope was to surprise it, for the road led to the rear of it. In case of failure, their position would be perilous in the extreme; and fail they surely would should accident or vigilance apprise the enemy of the movement.

II

The sleeping sentinel in the clump of laurel was a young Virginian named Carter Druse. He was the son of wealthy parents, an only child, and had known such ease and cultivation and high living as wealth and taste were able to command in the mountain country of western Virginia. His home was but a few miles from where he now lay. One morning he had risen from the breakfast-table and said, quietly but gravely: "Father, a Union regiment has arrived at Grafton. I am going to join it."

The father lifted his leonine head, looked at the son a moment in silence, and replied: "Well, go, sir, and whatever may occur do what you conceive to be your duty. Virginia, to which you are a traitor, must get on without you. Should we both live to the end of the war, we will speak further of the matter. Your mother, as the physician has informed you, is in a most critical condition; at the best she cannot be with us longer than a few weeks, but that time is precious. It would be better not to disturb her."

So Carter Druse, bowing reverently to his father, who returned the salute with a stately courtesy that masked a breaking heart, left the home of his childhood to go soldiering. By conscience and courage, by deeds of devotion and daring, he soon commended himself to his fellows and his officers; and it was to these qualities and to some knowledge of the country that he owed his selection for his present perilous duty at the extreme outpost. Nevertheless, fatigue had been stronger than resolution and he had fallen asleep. What good or bad angel came in a dream to rouse him from his state of crime, who shall say? Without a movement, without a sound, in the profound silence and the languor of the late afternoon, some invisible messenger of fate touched with unsealing finger the eyes of his consciousness — whispered into the ear of his spirit the mysterious awakening word which no human lips ever have spoken, no human memory ever has recalled. He quietly raised his forehead from his arm and looked between the masking stems of the laurels, instinctively closing his right hand about the stock of his rifle.

His first feeling was a keen artistic delight. On a colossal pedestal, the cliff, — motionless at the extreme edge of the capping rock and sharply outlined against the sky, — was an equestrian statue of impressive dignity. The figure of the man sat the figure of the horse, straight and soldierly, but with the repose of a Grecian god carved in the marble which limits the suggestion of activity. The gray costume harmonized with its aërial background; the metal of accoutrement and caparison was softened and subdued by the shadow; the animal's skin had no points of high light. A carbine strikingly foreshortened lay across the pommel of the saddle, kept in place by the right hand grasping it at the "grip"; the left hand, holding the bridle rein, was invisible. In silhouette against the sky the profile of the horse was cut with the sharpness of a cameo; it looked across the heights of air to the confronting cliffs beyond. The face of the rider, turned slightly away, showed only an outline of temple and beard; he was looking downward to the bottom of the valley. Magnified by its lift against the sky and by the soldier's testifying sense of the formidableness of a near enemy the group appeared of heroic, almost colossal, size.

For an instant Druse had a strange, half-defined feeling that he had slept to the end of the war and was looking upon a noble work of art reared upon that eminence to commemorate the deeds of an heroic past of which he had been an inglorious part. The feeling was dispelled by a slight movement of the group: the horse, without moving its feet, had drawn its body slightly backward from the verge; the man remained immobile as before. Broad awake and keenly alive to the significance of the situation, Druse now brought the butt of his rifle against his cheek by cautiously pushing the barrel forward through the bushes, cocked the piece, and glancing through the sights covered a vital spot of the horseman's breast. A touch upon the trigger and all would have been well with Carter Druse. At that instant the horseman turned his head and looked in the direction of his concealed foeman — seemed to look into his very face, into his eyes, into his brave, compassionate heart.

Is it then so terrible to kill an enemy in war — an enemy who has surprised a secret vital to the safety of one's self and comrades — an enemy more formidable for his knowledge than all his army for its numbers? Carter Druse grew pale; he shook in every limb, turned faint, and saw the statuesque group before him as black figures, rising, falling, moving unsteadily in arcs of circles in a fiery sky. His hand fell away from his weapon, his head slowly dropped until his face rested on the leaves in which he lay. This courageous gentleman and hardy soldier was near swooning from intensity of emotion.

It was not for long; in another moment his face was raised from earth, his hands resumed their places on the rifle, his forefinger sought the trigger; mind, heart, and eyes were clear, conscience and reason sound. He could not hope to capture that enemy; to alarm him would but send him dashing to his camp with his fatal news. The duty of the soldier was plain: the man must be shot dead from ambush — without warning, without a moment's spiritual preparation, with never so much as an unspoken prayer, he must be sent to his account. But no — there is a hope; he may have discovered nothing — perhaps he is but admiring the sublimity of the landscape. If permitted, he may turn and ride carelessly away in the direction whence he came. Surely it will be possible to judge at the instant of his withdrawing whether he knows. It may well be that his fixity of attention — Druse turned his head and looked through the deeps of air downward, as from the surface to the bottom of a translucent sea. He saw creeping across the green meadow a sinuous line of figures of men and horses — some foolish commander was permitting the soldiers of his escort to water their beasts in the open, in plain view from a dozen summits!

Druse withdrew his eyes from the valley and fixed them again upon the group of man and horse in the sky, and again it was through the sights of his rifle. But this time his aim was at the horse. In his memory, as if they were a divine mandate, rang the words of his father at their parting: "Whatever may occur, do what you conceive to be your duty." He was calm now. His teeth were firmly but not rigidly closed; his nerves were as tranquil as a sleeping babe's — not a tremor affected any muscle of his body; his breathing, until suspended in the act of taking aim, was regular and slow. Duty had conquered; the spirit had said to the body: "Peace, be still." He fired.

III

An officer of the Federal force, who in a spirit of adventure or in quest of knowledge had left the hidden bivouac in the valley, and with aimless feet had made his way to the lower edge of a small open space near the foot of the cliff, was considering what he had to gain by pushing his exploration further. At a distance of a quarter-mile before him, but apparently at a stone's throw, rose from its fringe of pines the gigantic face of rock, towering to so great a height above him that it made him giddy to look up to where its edge cut a sharp, rugged line against the sky. It presented a clean, vertical profile against a background of blue sky to a point half the way down, and of distant hills, hardly less blue, thence to the tops of the trees at its base. Lifting his eyes to the dizzy altitude of its summit the officer saw an astonishing sight — a man on horseback riding down into the valley through the air!

Straight upright sat the rider, in military fashion, with a firm seat in the saddle, a strong clutch upon the rein to hold his charger from too impetuous a plunge. From his bare head his long hair streamed upward, waving like a plume. His hands were concealed in the cloud of the horse's lifted mane. The animal's body was as level as if every hoof-stroke encountered the resistant earth. Its motions were those of a wild gallop, but even as the officer looked they ceased, with all the legs thrown sharply forward as in the act of alighting from a leap. But this was a flight!

Filled with amazement and terror by this apparition of a horseman in the sky — half believing himself the chosen scribe of some new Apocalypse, the officer was overcome by the intensity of his emotions; his legs failed him and he fell. Almost at the same instant he heard a crashing sound in the trees — a sound that died without an echo — and all was still.

The officer rose to his feet, trembling. The familiar sensation of an abraded shin recalled his dazed faculties. Pulling himself together he ran rapidly obliquely away from the cliff to a point distant from its foot; thereabout he expected to find his man; and thereabout he naturally failed. In the fleeting instant of his vision his imagination had been so wrought upon by the apparent grace and ease and intention of the marvelous performance that it did not occur to him that the line of march of aërial cavalry is directly downward, and that he could find the objects of his search at the very foot of the cliff. A half-hour later he returned to camp.

This officer was a wise man; he knew better than to tell an incredible truth. He said nothing of what he had seen. But when the commander asked him if in his scout he had learned anything of advantage to the expedition he answered:

"Yes, sir; there is no road leading down into this valley from the southward."

The commander, knowing better, smiled.

IV

After firing his shot, Private Carter Druse reloaded his rifle and resumed his watch. Ten minutes had hardly passed when a Federal sergeant crept cautiously to him on hands and knees. Druse neither turned his head nor looked at him, but lay without motion or sign of recognition.

"Did you fire?" the sergeant whispered.

"Yes."

"At what?"

"A horse. It was standing on yonder rock — pretty far out. You see it is no longer there. It went over the cliff."

The man's face was white, but he showed no other sign of emotion. Having answered, he turned away his eyes and said no more. The sergeant did not understand.

"See here, Druse," he said, after a moment's silence, "it's no use making a mystery. I order you to report. Was there anybody on the horse?"

"Yes."

"Well?"

"My father."

The sergeant rose to his feet and walked away. "Good God!" he said.

THE MIND OF THE HORSE

We've spoken of herds and instinct, and despite millennia of interaction we still have only a general concept of the unknown, the unspoken, the unfathomed intelligence of wild animals. There's no telling how intelligent wolves and coyotes are. But look at the way they observe and how they adapt. We know that birds, especially the corvid family, are very intelligent. Parrots too, and of course, dolphins. There is an intelligence in all animals that human beings, for the most part, are too arrogant to see.

The horse-human relationship uplifts the intelligence of both. I don't mean "learning," of course, but "wisdom." I think it is really significant that the Buddha has this term, "dependent co-arising." Buddha rode a horse, Kanthaka, and he understood — perhaps based a lot of his thinking on the fact — that they mutually uplifted each other, that there was this cycle of one causing the other to rise beyond instinct and into a stage of deeper interaction.

We have discussed, and will continue to talk about, this idea of equine intelligence. But while that is a little-understood reality, the idea is supported by its darker side: horse sociopathy.

There are isolated cases, for example, of psychotic horses that hold a grudge.

I know a story of a great trainer, Tom Moore, who was attacked in a stall by a stallion, almost killed. At the last minute a groom came in and used a pitchfork to push the stallion off, and Tom was saved. Moore sold the stallion. Years later, Tom was judging a show hundreds of miles away, and in comes the horse, who has now been gelded and was in a competition with a rider on his back. The horse saw Tom and ran at him to attack. The horse had to be withdrawn, immediately.

I don't know whether, unbeknownst to Tom, that horse was beaten or whether it was born crazy. Like some people, there are psychopathic horses. There is no rehabilitating the animals and they must invariably be put down before they can harm a human or another horse.

It's interesting, though, that an animal that is in no way a predator should have a brain that has the capacity to focus its rage or hate or madness. Especially if it isn't being challenged for leadership in any way.

Perhaps we should call this the dichotomy of the horse or the horse with two faces. I don't know. I *do* know that alone among all the animals, the horse had unique qualities that ancient peoples did not have the time or capacity to understand. I hope one day that we do, because it will almost certainly lead to a greater understanding of our own darker sides.

MR. STIVER'S HORSE

The Wit and Humor of America, Vol. 3,
BY JAMES MONTGOMERY BAILEY (1907)

Shortly after serving in the Civil War, James Montgomery Bailey (1841–1894) returned to Connecticut, where he founded a newspaper, the revered *Danbury News.* He wrote articles, he wrote books — and he wrote this tale, which appears to be his sole foray into the topic of horses. It is another tale that demonstrates little ways in which most of the time, to a horse — intelligence and empathy notwithstanding — the horse comes first.

The other morning at breakfast Mrs. Perkins observed that Mr. Stiver, in whose house we live, had been called away, and wanted to know if I would see to his horse through the day.

I knew that Mr. Stiver owned a horse, because I occasionally saw him drive out of the yard, and I saw the stable every day — but what kind of a horse I didn't know. I never went into the stable, for two reasons: in the first place, I had no desire to; and, secondly, I didn't know as the horse cared particularly for company.

I never took care of a horse in my life;

and, had I been of a less hopeful nature, the charge Mr. Stiver had left with me might have had a very depressing effect; but I told Mrs. Perkins I would do it.

"You know how to take care of a horse, don't you?" said she.

I gave her a reassuring wink. In fact, I knew so little about it that I didn't think it safe to converse more fluently than by winks.

After breakfast I seized a toothpick and walked out towards the stable. There was nothing particular to do, as Stiver had given him his breakfast, and I found him eating it; so I looked around. The horse looked around, too, and stared pretty hard at me. There was but little said on either side. I hunted up the location of the feed, and then sat down on a peck measure and fell to studying the beast. There is a wide difference in horses. Some of them will kick you over and never look around to see what becomes of you. I don't like a disposition like that, and I wondered if Stiver's horse was one of them.

When I came home at noon I went straight to the stable. The animal was there all right. Stiver hadn't told me what to give him for dinner, and I had not given the subject any thought; but I went to the oat-box and filled the peck measure and sallied boldly up to the manger.

When he saw the oats he almost smiled; this pleased and amused him. I emptied them into the trough, and left him above me to admire the way I parted my hair behind. I just got my head up in time to save the whole of it. He had his ears back, his mouth open, and looked as if he were on the point of committing murder. I went out and filled the measure again, and climbed up the side of the stall and emptied it on top of him. He brought his head up so suddenly at this that I immediately got down, letting go of everything to do it. I struck on the sharp edge of a barrel, rolled over a couple of times, then disappeared under a hay-cutter. The peck measure went down on the other side, and got mysteriously tangled up in that animal's heels, and he went to work at it, and then ensued the most dreadful noise I ever heard in all my life, and I have been married eighteen years.

It did seem as if I never would get out from under that hay-cutter; and all the while I was struggling and wrenching myself and the cutter apart, that awful beast was kicking around in the stall, and making the most appalling sound imaginable.

When I got out I found Mrs. Perkins at

the door. She had heard the racket, and had sped out to the stable, her only thought being of me and three stove-lids which she had under her arm, and one of which she was about to fire at the beast.

This made me mad.

"Go away, you unfortunate idiot!" I shouted: "do you want to knock my brains out?" For I remembered seeing Mrs. Perkins sling a missile once before, and that I nearly lost an eye by the operation, although standing on the other side of the house at the time.

She retired at once. And at the same time the animal quieted down, but there was nothing left of that peck measure, not even the maker's name.

I followed Mrs. Perkins into the house, and had her do me up, and then I sat down in a chair and fell into a profound strain of meditation. After a while I felt better, and went out to the stable again. The horse was leaning against the stable stall, with eyes half closed, and appeared to be very much engrossed in thought.

"Step off to the left," I said, rubbing his back.

He didn't step. I got the pitchfork and punched him in the leg with the handle. He immediately raised up both hind legs at once, and that fork flew out of my hands, and went rattling up against the timbers above, and came down again in an instant, the end of the handle rapping me with such force on the top of the head that I sat right down on the floor under the impression that I was standing in front of a drug-store in the evening. I went back to the house and got some more stuff on me. But I couldn't keep away from that stable. I went out there again. The thought struck me that what the horse wanted was exercise. If that thought had been an empty glycerin-can, it would have saved a windfall of luck for me.

But exercise would tone him down, and exercise him I should. I laughed to myself to think how I would trounce him around the yard. I didn't laugh again that afternoon. I got him unhitched, and then wondered how I was to get him out of the stall without carrying him out. I pushed, but he wouldn't budge. I stood looking at him in the face, thinking of something to say, when he suddenly solved the difficulty by veering about and plunging for the door. I followed, as a matter of course, because I had a tight hold on the rope, and hit about every partition-stud worth speaking of on that side of the barn. Mrs. Perkins was at the window and saw us come out of the door. She subsequently remarked that we came out skipping like two innocent children. The skipping was entirely unintentional on my part. I felt as if I stood on the verge of eternity. My legs may have skipped, but my mind was filled with awe.

I took the animal out to exercise him. He exercised me before I got through with it. He went around a few times in a circle; then he stopped suddenly, spread out his forelegs, and looked at me. Then he leaned forward a little, and hoisted both hind legs, and threw about two coal-hods of mud over a line full of clothes Mrs. Perkins had just hung out.

That excellent lady had taken a position at the window, and, whenever the evolutions of the awful beast permitted, I caught a glance of her features. She appeared to be very much interested in the proceedings; but the instant that the mud flew, she disappeared from the window, and a moment later she appeared on the stoop with a long poker in her hand, and fire enough in her eye to heat it red-hot.

Just then Stiver's horse stood up on his hind legs and tried to hug me with the others. This scared me. A horse never shows his strength to such advantage as when he is coming down on you like a frantic pile-driver. I instantly dodged, and the cold sweat fairly boiled out of me.

It suddenly came over me that I had once figured in a similar position years ago. My grandfather owned a little white horse that would get up from a meal at Delmonico's to kick the President of the United States. He sent me to the lot one day, and unhappily suggested that I often went after that horse and suffered all kinds of defeat in getting him out of the pasture, but I had never tried to ride him. Heaven knows I never thought of it. I had my usual trouble with him that day. He tried to jump over me, and push me down in a mud-hole, and finally got up on his hind legs and came waltzing after me with facilities enough to convert me into hash, but I turned and just made for that fence with all the agony a prospect of instant death could crowd into me. If our candidate for the Presidency had run one-half as well, there would be seventy-five postmasters in Danbury to-day, instead of one.

I got him out finally, and then he was quiet enough, and I took him up alongside the fence and got on him. He stopped an instant, one brief instant, and then tore off down the road at a frightful speed. I lay down on him and clasped my hands tightly around his neck, and thought of my home. When we got to the stable I was confident he would stop, but he didn't. He drove straight at the door. It was a low door, just high enough to permit him to go in at lightning speed, but there was no room for me. I saw if I struck that stable the struggle would be a very brief one. I thought this all over in an instant, and then, spreading out my arms and legs, emitted a scream, and the next moment I was bounding about in the filth of that stable-yard. All this passed through my mind as Stiver's horse went up into the air. It frightened Mrs. Perkins dreadfully.

"Why, you old fool!" she said; "why don't you get rid of him?"

"How can I?" said I, in desperation.

"Why, there are a thousand ways," said she.

This is just like a woman. How differently a statesman would have answered!

But I could think of only two ways to dispose of the beast. I could either swallow him where he stood and then sit down on him, or I could crawl inside of him and kick him to death.

But I was saved either of these expedients by his coming towards me so abruptly that I dropped the rope in terror, and then he turned about, and, kicking me full of mud, shot for the gate, ripping the clothes-line in two, and went on down the street at a horrible gallop, with two of Mrs. Perkins' garments, which he hastily snatched from the line, floating over his neck in a very picturesque manner.

So I was afterwards told. I was too full of mud myself to see the way into the house.

Stiver got his horse all right, and stays at home to care for him. Mrs. Perkins has gone to her mother's to recuperate, and I am healing as fast as possible.

The Horse as Hero . . . Not

I mentioned Gene Autry and other movie and TV cowboys previously. Bless their well-meaning hearts, they, along with many of the authors I've read while finding stories for this book, have perpetuated an enduring, loving, but absolutely wrong idea about horses. I'll get to that in a moment.

Having spent a lot of time around horses, both as an actor and as an owner/breeder/rider, I know something about the animal. And I'm here to disabuse you of a notion that crosses both my film and real-life experiences: do not believe what you see on-screen and on TV or read in wonderful adventure stories. Horses are magnificent, they are at times brave, but they are not heroic. And by that I mean, I do not think that horses recognize a human being in trouble. They will not gallop to their rescue, as we've seen Silver do for the Lone Ranger.

It's true that they recognize that the human being is acting in a different manner — for example, if they're writhing in pain or screaming in fear or breathless with a heart attack. But they would not recognize the human as being in trouble, so much as they would recognize the human acting in an aberrant way. The horse having made that determination, there are two possible results. First, it may frighten the horse. Or second, it will make the horse curious. That second option will lead back to the first — or else a third option: they will not be fearful but will continue doing whatever they were doing. None of which helps the stricken or endangered rider unless someone schooled in horses happens to notice the animal acting strangely.

To my knowledge, horses have never really placed themselves in front of danger as perceived by the horse — keeping in mind the horse wouldn't necessarily recognize a bullet or a knife as dangerous. They would just know attitudes. For example, they would instinctively recognize a predator. They may never have seen a lion, or a tiger, or a really big cat, but their intuition would be to flee that scent and that sound. Also snakes. They'll react to the motion, the sound. They may, in their panic, rear and come down on an enemy, frighten it away.

But whatever instinct has been bred through a million years, the ones who react to danger the right way — by flight — survive. And the ones who don't react by running off, or who are so panicked they run down a dangerous slope — they do not survive.

By comparison, dogs are different. I've had one or more dogs every year of my adult life. I've had tens of dogs. Dogs are not herbivores: they are territorial carnivores. When a dog is part of your family, part of your pack, it considers you the alpha dog. It expects you to do the heavy lifting: feeding, walking, grooming . . . protecting. And if there is a perceived threat, and the dog barks or bites, what is being expressed is actually aggressive behavior based on fear. However, the dog will also protect you, protect the pack, protect their territory to the death.

So in real life, if fictional young dog owner Joe Carraclough fell in a river, chances are pretty good Lassie would jump in and attempt to save him. If a squirrel came by at the same time, the dog might be *tempted* to chase it, but the safety of the master would come first. Meanwhile, if Roy Rogers fell from Trigger in a prairie fire, Roy would be on his own. Trigger would not gallop for help. He would not pull Roy out by his teeth. He would get away from the blaze.

Eons have evolved an animal that lives in apprehension of everything around it. And that's one of the beauties of a horse, in that the horse is in the moment. Because it needs to be. We do not believe it will think or reason. It has no comprehension of what happened in the past, nor the ability to perceive of the future. It lives in the now, and that's a huge lesson for human beings.

I love them all, horse and dog, just the same. But if I'm in trouble, and my dog can't help me, *then* I'll be calling 911.

Yet, all that being said, my good friend the author Linda Kohanov tells of spending time with a horse to which she was really bonded who got injured and couldn't be ridden to any great extent. Linda spent time with her, taking her for long walks in the desert. The horse became so acclimatized to doing this that Linda would take the leading rope off, and started taking her dog out with them. Well, one time they ran into a herd of longhorn cattle that came out of nowhere and were disturbingly interested in the uncommon trio. The cattle started walking toward the group, with these long horns and really intense looks on their faces. Linda says that she expected the dog would chase them off, or that she would need to take a

165

lead rope and scare them off, or just kind of slink away quietly and try not to be stampeded or skewered with their horns.

What happened was that while the dog ran and stood shivering against her leg, the lame horse stepped out and herded those cattle away from them: she put herself between Linda and the cattle, and she was not even an experienced cow horse.

Linda says that this was the first and only time she felt that this idea of horses as quivering gutless victims, always ready to run off, was turned upside down.

One could say that the horse was protecting itself, or briefly joining the larger herd, or even maternally looking after that herd. We cannot know for sure. But if the horse was looking out for its companions, then perhaps we are witnessing the first glimmers of a change in evolutionary behavior brought on by centuries of human-horse bonding.

Don't Look a Gift-Horse in the Mouth

Verse and Worse,
BY HARRY GRAHAM (1905)

Mr. Graham (1874–1936) was a Renaissance man. Soldier, journalist, poet, lyricist, translator, and humorist, he was also engaged to one of the leading actresses of his day: Ethel Barrymore. When he did marry, he had a daughter — Virginia Graham — who became a humorist in her own right.

I have to confess, I laughed out loud when I first read this one, which not only addresses horses having self-protective horse sense, but also some of the most ancient wisdom known to humankind. Though I also have to admit that the challenge of anthologizing in some ways mirrors the megrims of the Internet, where it is impossible to verify certain things that are written and said. There was some debate among us about one word in this light verse: the printed edition says "servant's tooth" and it is impossible to know whether that was a typo meant to reference the line in *King Lear* about a "serpent's tooth" or a play on Shakespeare's words. We left it as we found it, though the consensus is that this version is in error.

I knew a man who lived down South;
He thought this maxim to defy;
He looked a Gift-horse in the Mouth;
The Gift-horse bit him in the Eye!
And, while the steed enjoyed his bite,
My Southern friend mislaid his sight.
Now, had this foolish man, that day,
Observed the Gift-horse in the Heel,
It might have kicked his brains away,
But that's a loss he would not feel;
Because, you see (need I explain?),
My Southern friend has got no brain.
When any one to you presents
A poodle, or a pocket-knife,
A set of Ping-pong instruments,
A banjo or a lady-wife,
'Tis churlish, as I understand,
To grumble that they're second-hand.
And he who termed Ingratitude
As "worser nor a servant's tooth"
Was evidently well imbued
With all the elements of Truth;
(While he who said "Uneasy lies
The tooth that wears a crown" was wise).
"One must be poor," George Eliot said,
"To know the luxury of giving";
So too one really should be dead
To realise the joy of living.

(I'd sooner be — I don't know which —
I'd like to be alive and rich!)
This book may be a Gift-horse too,
And one you surely ought to prize;
If so, I beg you, read it through,
With kindly and uncaptious eyes,
Not grumbling because this particular line
    doesn't happen to scan,
And this one doesn't rhyme!

MY GREAT DAY

I would like to share with you where my love affair with horses *truly* started. Not just as a kid talking his way onto a horse's back, or riding in the movies, but the real deal. The passion, the deep and profound communion, the road to enlightenment about the horse, myself, and the universe we live in.

It began with my beloved horse Great Day, a relationship that would constitute and define a large part of my life and of my life with horses. I have owned many other wonderful horses — for example, Harley, so-named because it allowed me to tell people I was riding one; and the exceptional All Glory, a renowned trotting horse who my wife, Elizabeth, rode to many championships. But Great Day was special and to explain why will require a number of digressions and divertissements . . . starting, in fact, right at the top.

American Saddlebreds are proud, sturdy creatures. To this point, they have been used in war many times, the most expansive of which was the Civil War. A horse in war is facing gunfire and explosions and shouts and cries of other horses and riders — sounds that would rightfully terrify anybody. These horses face sabers swinging by their eyes, whips cracking here and there, mud and blood splattering their flanks, bullets striking other horses, other riders, crashing in their field of view. There is also the physical stress imposed by those same riders attempting to physically enlarge themselves by standing up in the stirrups and screaming to their men to move onward, forward, attack!

Even if you can desensitize horses to that, there's still the unexpected. Thunder and lightning. Wind.

Elephants.

Not in the Civil War, of course, but the commander from Carthage, Hannibal who, in 218 BCE worked to get as many elephants over the Alps as possible, because he knew that the warhorses of Rome would be frightened by the appearance and sound of the elephant. And when he managed to get those few that he did across the mountains, it delivered the early success he enjoyed

171

against the Roman legions: the horses turned 180 degrees and flew.

Many otherwise rational human beings have that reaction in their first experience with war. They become panicked and run away like any wild animal.

So the Saddlebred was bred to do the best that any horse can do under warlike conditions.

Enter me and *T. J. Hooker.*

I shot this series in Hollywood from 1982 to 1986. During that time we filmed an episode involving a racetrack heist called "Homecoming." We went to a barn in Los Angeles that we were using as a location for a chase scene. And we drove up and down the stall way, the pathways around the stalls, me in a cop car after the bad guy. For the most part, these Saddlebreds reacted with curiosity, as opposed to ramming their heads against the stall in order to get away. That intrigued me.

At that time, I had no knowledge of their iron constitutions, relative to many horses. And, of course, though I was getting knocked around in the car there were no screeching tires. The horses saw cars moving by, something that had a familiar fuel smell — and most likely they felt no threat. I don't know.

172

But between shots — when actors have a lot of time to learn lines or, in a chase scene, to do nothing — I looked at these beautiful, beautiful horses, and I fell in love. Not with one animal in particular, not yet. But with horses in general. Maybe that sense of wondrous freedom and accomplishment I had felt as a boy was stirred. Regardless, I decided to investigate horse ownership. Needless to say, my financial adviser and my business manager were both against it. They said, kidding but not kidding, "Don't buy anything that eats while you sleep."

Actually, buying horses was a process. I inadvertently laid the groundwork when I bought some land in central California, just with the idea of buying some land and living on it. I hired somebody to watch over the spread, and he lived in a house that was already on it while I built another house for us. After I shot that *T. J. Hooker* episode, the person who was living on the land said, "What else do you want to do with the land?" I asked him what he meant. "Well," he told me, "I could build some fences, and you could run a horse here." And I said, "That's a great idea, I've never had a horse." He said, "So happens there's an auction not far from here tomorrow, would you like to go to it?"

I thought: *Why not? It might be an interest-ing experience, just to watch the process.*

So he and I go to the auction, and there we meet a friend of his who has a son named Philip. And Philip is about twelve years old — kismet? — the age I was when I first rode a horse. And he knows more about horses than the three other adults combined. So I sit beside Philip, and Philip says, "Oh, look at this horse that's up there now. You should buy this horse. He's perfect for you."

And I look at the animal, knowing noth-ing other than that he's a three-year-old horse. That's not a lot of information for a novice, and as the auction's going on I raise my hand to Philip and say no with my hand. Whereupon the auctioneer says, "Sold, to William Shatner, for the price of —"

I had inadvertently bought a horse. And I was torn between saying "No, no, I didn't mean to —" and embarrassing myself that way, or saying to myself, "All right, screw it, I bought a horse. That's what I came here for, right?" Well, not *really.* I'd been think-ing about it. It just happened sooner than I planned with me having done absolutely no due diligence.

But I'm an optimist. I thought, *Maybe it'll work out.*

174

As they say today, it *so* did. It was a wonderful quarter horse and I enjoyed riding him, as bad, as unschooled, as awkward as I was. And that begat a whole network of horses and farms.

Very quickly, I became involved with horse people from Kentucky, because Saddlebreds are most popular in the South and most popular in Kentucky. They are synonymous. Saddlebreds exist in other states as well, of course, but the center of the industry for the last two hundred years has been Kentucky. I arrived in Kentucky and fell in love with the whole Kentucky Saddlebred industry.

As soon as I arrived — perhaps it was fate — I was introduced to a very young black colt. I was swept away. Unlike with my first purchase, the magnificence of *that* horse struck me at once. It had to have been the way Alexander the Great felt about Bucephalus. *Had* to be.

That was how the two-year-old Great Day came into my life. I overpaid for him — I didn't know that I should have guarded my celebrity, my inexperience, not that it would have mattered: I had to have him.

A year later we won the three-year-old world championship in harness. What that means is, you ride in a two-wheeled rig behind him. The horse is so beautiful in his animation that you don't want to put a rider on his back to offend his line of conformation. You want the totality of his beauty for people to see. He's a work of art. He's descended from top English racehorses and has been worked on for two centuries, bred by knowledgeable people who devote their lives to breeding the finest of these horses.

After I won that world championship, me and my trainer, we made him into a breeding horse. Because he was a breeding horse he could no longer compete, really, because now his interest — quite understandably — was in breeding and not in performance. And during this period he became more and more "rank," as we call it in the horse business — he became more and more difficult.

"Where are you taking me to? I hope you're taking me to a mare. This isn't a mare, this is a rider! I want a mare!"

And so a struggle would erupt, and I lost him not just as a competitor but as a friend, because he was stud-like in his behavior, which meant he would nip, he would bite . . . he could, in fact, be dangerous. And when I took him out to graze we always had a groom beside me because Great Day would do little mutterings, little grunts and groans, and you could see that he wanted to breed. And he was wondering where that mare was. That became very, very obvious, if you get my meaning.

It was difficult for him and for me to watch him grow so very, very emotional, very high, hot-blooded. And the older he got, the more of a stud horse he became. Which meant that at times he would kick, he would paw, and he would bite himself. So as to make that less hazardous for him, they would use kicking chains on his back feet, which became pawing chains on his front feet, and eventually poles that led to a bit in his mouth and poles strapped to his sides so that he wouldn't savage himself, gnaw himself — just as a caged parrot might, from frustration and rage, pluck its feathers out. Because they do need others. They're flock animals, herd animals.

To understand that more precisely, consider the difference of a horse in the wild. The standard there is for a stallion to work twenty-four hours a day — breeding, defending, and helping to lead the herd into safety.

In civilization, they're in a stall by themselves for twenty-three and a half hours a day, and if they were not accustomed to that — even if they are — it can lead to destruction.

I didn't know that, and I didn't seek good advice. And gradually, as they put more and more appliances on this horse to prevent him from hurting himself, the more guilt I felt for having put Great Day into this position. That horse was in solitary confinement, eventually. And I grieved over it.

I took him to live in Belle Reve, my beautiful, bucolic place located in the foothills of the Sierras. It is a place of great meaning for the Shatner family. My late wife Nerine and Elizabeth's late husband Mike are there, and it is where my wife Elizabeth and I will be as well. Native Americans lived and camped on that land for generations.

There came a time, of course, when there was no more fight left in that magnificent creature. He died on March 20, 2004 — two days shy of his twenty-third birthday. Here is part of what I wrote at that time about Great Day upon his passing:

On a warm, spring afternoon, I led Great Day into a shady dell for his last hour with me. For a while I spent the time watching him graze, connected to a lead shank. It was peaceful and for the first time in years, I was bonding with him. I was anticipating and even dreading the moment when the vet would arrive to give him his final shots.

All of a sudden, from across the field, three horses came running. Great Day raised up and then in a flash, the stallion of old, the great protector of the herd, Great Day's instincts took hold. On feeble rear legs, he reared, pawing the air with bandaged front feet, neighing his defiance. The other horses turned tail and ran. Great Day settled back down, defiant and proud, as someone remarked later. He went into the next world feeling like a stud horse.

I miss him, still, though I often go to visit. He is buried in land that was occupied for hundreds of years by Native Americans. There's all kinds of relics still there, left where we found them, which include a pestle and mortar for acorns, and of course the water where they fished and drank. I have spirit statues all over the land. I had a craftsman make spirit statues of the wolf and the bear and the eagle. This land is very spiritual. People that I invite to come up there, they cry out of joy for what they experience, and Great Day is part of the spirit of this land.

Thank you, Great Day, for all the memories past . . . and present.

Samuel Cowles and His Horse Royal

Second Book of Tales,
BY EUGENE FIELD (1911)

Here's a tale of boyhood from Eugene Field. In his too-short life (1850–1895), Field was a renowned American journalist who also wrote poems and short stories for children. The most famous of his works is the delightful "Wynken, Blynken, and Nod," about a trio who went sailing in a wooden shoe.

I found nothing in his biography to reflect any extensive association with horses. However, with a reporter's practiced eye and ear he certainly picked up a great deal in the Midwestern environs in which he lived.

The day on which I was twelve years old my father said to me: "Samuel, walk down the lane with me to the pasture-lot; I want to show you something." Never suspicioning anything, I trudged along with father, and what should I find in the pasture-lot but the cunningest, prettiest, liveliest colt a boy ever clapped eyes on!

"That is my birthday present to you," said father. "Yes, Samuel, I give the colt to you to do with as you like, for you've been a good boy and have done well at school."

You can easily understand that my boyish heart overflowed with pride and joy and gratitude. A great many years have elapsed since that time, but I haven't forgotten and I never shall forget the delight of that moment, when I realized that I had a colt of my own — a real, live colt, and a Morgan colt, at that!

"How old is he, father?" I asked.

"A week old, come to-morrow," said father.

"Has Judge Phipps seen him yet?" I asked.

"No; nobody has seen him but you and me and the hired man."

Judge Phipps was the justice of the peace. I had a profound respect for him, for what he didn't know about horses wasn't worth knowing; I was sure of this, because the judge himself told me so. One of the first duties to which I applied myself was to go and get the judge and show him the colt. The judge praised the pretty creature inordinately, enumerating all his admirable points and predicting a famous career for him. The judge even went so far as to express the conviction that in due time my colt would win "imperishable renown and immortal laurels as a competitor at the meetings of the Hampshire County Trotting

Association," of which association the judge was the president, much to the scandal of his estimable wife, who viewed with pious horror her husband's connection with the race-track.

"What do you think I ought to name my colt?" I asked of the judge.

"When I was about your age," the judge answered, "I had a colt and I named him Royal. He won all the premiums at the county fair before he was six year old."

That was quite enough for me. To my thinking every utterance of the judge's was ex cathedra; moreover, in my boyish exuberance, I fancied that this name would start my colt auspiciously upon a famous career; I began at once to think and to speak of him as the prospective winner of countless honors.

From the moment when I first set eyes on Royal I was his stanch friend; even now, after the lapse of years, I cannot think of my old companion without feeling here in my breast a sense of gratitude that that honest, patient, loyal friend entered so largely into my earlier life.

Twice a day I used to trudge down the lane to the pasture-lot to look at the colt, and invariably I was accompanied by a troop of boy acquaintances who heartily envied me my good luck, and who regaled me constantly with suggestions of what they would do if Royal were their colt. Royal soon became friendly with us all, and he would respond to my call, whinnying to me as I came down the lane, as much as to say: "Good morning to you, little master! I hope you are coming to have a romp with me." And, gracious! how he would curve his tail and throw up his head and gather his short body together and trot around the pasture-lot on those long legs of his! He enjoyed life, Royal did, as much as we boys enjoyed it.

Naturally enough, I made all sorts of plans for Royal. I recall that, after I had been on a visit to Springfield and had beholden for the first time the marvels of Barnum's show, I made up my mind that when Royal and I were old enough we would unite our fortunes with those of a circus, and in my imagination I already pictured huge and gaudy posters announcing the blood-curdling performances of the dashing bareback equestrian, Samuel Cowles, upon his fiery Morgan steed, Royal! This plan was not at all approved of by Judge Phipps, who continued to insist that it was on the turf and not in the sawdust circle that Royal's genius lay, and to this way of thinking I was finally converted, but not until the judge had promised to give me a sulky as soon as Royal demonstrated his ability to make a mile in 2:40.

It is not without a sigh of regret that in my present narrative I pass over the five years next succeeding the date of Royal's arrival. For they were very happy years — indeed, at this distant period I am able to recall only that my boyhood was full, brimful of happiness. I broke Royal myself; father and the hired man stood around and made suggestions, and at times they presumed to take a hand in the proceedings. Virtually, however, I broke Royal to the harness and to the saddle, and after that I was even more attached to him than ever before — you know how it is, if ever you've broken a colt yourself!

When I went away to college it seemed to me that leaving Royal was almost as hard as leaving mother and father; you see the colt had become a very large part of my boyish life — followed me like a pet dog, was lonesome when I wasn't round, used to rub his nose against my arm and look lovingly at me out of his big, dark, mournful eyes — yes, I cried when I said good-by to him the morning I started for Williamstown. I was ashamed of it then, but not now — no, not now.

But my fun was all the keener, I guess, when I came home at vacation times. Then we had it, up hill and down dale — Royal and I did! In the summer-time along the narrow roads we trailed, and through leafy lanes, and in my exultation I would cut at the tall weeds at the roadside and whisk at the boughs arching overhead, as if I were a warrior mounted for battle and these other things were human victims to my valor. In the winter we sped away over the snow and ice, careless to the howling of the wind and the wrath of the storm. Royal knew the favorite road, every inch of the way; he knew, too, when Susie held the reins — Susie was Judge Phipps' niece, and I guess she'd have mittened me if it hadn't been that I had the finest colt in the county!

The summer I left college there came to me an overwhelming sense of patriotic duty. Mother was the first to notice my absent-mindedness, and to her I first confided the great wish of my early manhood. It is hard for parents to bid a son go forth to do service upon the battlefield, but New England in those times responded cheerfully and nobly to Mr. Lincoln's call. The Eighth Massachusetts cavalry was the regiment I enlisted in; a baker's dozen of us boys went together from the quiet little village nestling in the shadow of Mount Holyoke. From Camp Andrew I wrote back a piteous letter, complaining of the horse that had been assigned to me; I wanted Royal; we had been inseparable in times of peace — why should we not share together the fortunes of war? Within a fortnight along came Royal, conducted in all dignity by — you would never guess — by Judge Phipps! Full of patriotism and of cheer was the judge.

"Both of ye are thoroughbreds," said he. "Ye'll come in under the wire first every time, I know ye will."

The judge also brought me a saddle blanket which Susie had ornamented with wondrous and tender art.

So Royal and I went into the war together. There were times of privation and of danger; neither of us ever complained. I am proud to bear witness that in every emergency my horse bore himself with a patience and a valor that seemed actually human. My comrades envied me my gentle, stanch, obedient servant. Indeed, Royal and I became famous as inseparable and loyal friends.

We were in five battles and neither of us got even so much as a scratch. But one afternoon in a skirmish with the rebels near Potomac Mills a bullet struck me in the thigh, and from the mere shock I fell from Royal's back into the tangle of the thicket. The fall must have stunned me, for the next thing I knew I was alone — deserted of all except my faithful horse. Royal stood over me, and when I opened my eyes he gave a faint whinny. I hardly knew what to do. My leg pained me excruciatingly. I surmised that I would never be able to make my way back to camp under the fire of the rebel picketers, for I discovered that they were closing in.

Then it occurred to me to pin a note to Royal's saddle blanket and to send Royal back to camp telling the boys of the trouble I was in. The horse understood it all; off he galloped, conscious of the import of the mission upon which he had been dispatched. Bang-bang-bang! went the guns over yonder, as if the revengeful creatures in the far-off brush guessed the meaning of our manoeuvering and sought to slay my loyal friend. But not a bullet touched him — leastwise he galloped on and on till I lost sight of him. They came for me at last, the boys did; they were a formidable detachment, and how the earth shook as they swept along!

"We thought you were a goner, sure," said Hi Bixby.

"I guess I would have been if it hadn't been for Royal," said I.

"I guess so, myself," said he. "When we saw him stumblin' along all bloody we allowed for sure you was dead!"

"All bloody?" I cried. "Is Royal hurt?"

"As bad as a hoss can be," said he.

In camp we found them doing the best they could for him. But it was clearly of no avail. There was a gaping, ragged hole in his side; seeking succor for me, Royal had met his death-wound. I forgot my own hurt; I thrust the others aside and hobbled where he lay.

"Poor old Roy!" I cried, as I threw myself beside my dying friend and put my arms about his neck. Then I patted and stroked him and called him again and again by name, and there was a look in his eyes that told me he knew me and was glad that I was there.

How strange, and yet how beautiful, it was that in that far-off country, with my brave, patient, loyal friend's fluttering heart close unto mine, I neither saw nor thought of the scene around me.

But before my eyes came back the old, familiar places — the pasture-lot, the lane, the narrow road up the hill, the river winding along between great stretches of brown corn, the aisle of maple trees, and the fountain where we drank so many, many times together — and I smelled the fragrance of the flowers and trees abloom, and I heard the dear voices and the sweet sounds of my boyhood days.

Then presently a mighty shudder awakened me from this dreaming. And I cried out with affright and grief, for I felt that I was alone.

To Horse

Life's Minor Collisions,
BY FRANCES AND GERTRUDE WARNER
(1921)

Gertrude Warner is best known for her enduring children's series The Boxcar Children. She coauthored this story with her older sister — for adults. It appeared in a wonderful collection that I read in its entirety when I should have been perusing horse tales!

"A duck," we used to read in the primer at school, "a duck is a long low animal covered with feathers." Similarly, a horse is a long high animal, covered with confusion. This applies to the horse as we find him in the patriotic Parade, where a brass-band precedes him, an unaccustomed rider surmounts him, and a drum-corps brings up his rear.

In our own Welcome Home Parade, after the boys returned from France, the Legion decided to double the number of its mounted effectives: all the overseas officers should ride. All the overseas officers were instantly on their feet. Their protests were loud and heated. A horse, they said, was something that they personally had never bestridden. They offered to ride anything else. They would fly down the avenue in Spads, or do the falling leaf over the arch of triumph. They would ride tanks or motor-cycles or army-trucks. But a horse was a thing of independent locomotion, not to be trifled with. It was not the idea of getting killed that they objected to, it was the looks of the thing. By "the thing," they meant not the horse, but the rider.

In spite of the veto of the officers, the mo-tion was carried by acclamation. The mediæval charm of a mounted horse-guard instantly kindled the community imagina-tion. The chaplain, fresh from the navy, was promised a milk-white palfrey for his espe-cial use, if he would wear his ice-cream suit for the occasion.

There was no time to practise before the event, but the boys were told to give them-selves no anxiety about mounts. Well-bred and competent horses would appear punc-tually just before the time for falling in. The officers were instructed to go to a certain corner of a side street, find the fence behind the garage where the animals would be tied, select their favorite form of horse from the collection they would see there, and ride him up to the green.

When Geoffrey came home and said that

he was to ride a horse in the procession, our mother, who had been a good horsewoman in her girlhood, took him aside and gave him a few quiet tips. Some horses, she said, had been trained to obey certain signals, and some to obey the exact opposite. For instance, some would go faster if you reined them in, and some would slow down. Some waited for light touches from their master's hand or foot, and others for their master's voice. You had to study your horse as an individual.

Geoffrey said that he was glad to hear any little inside gossip of this sort, and made his way alone to the place appointed, skilfully dodging friends. We gathered that if he had to have an interview with a horse, he preferred to have it with nobody looking on.

The fence behind the garage was fringed with horses securely tied, and the top of the fence was fringed with a row of small boys, waiting. Geoffrey approached the line of horses, and glanced judicially down the row. Books on "Reading Character at Sight" make a great point of the distinctions between blond and brunette, the concave and the convex profile, the glance of the eye, and the manner of shaking hands. Geoffrey could tell at a glance that the handshake of these horses would be firm and full of decision. As one man they turned and looked at him, and their eyes were level and inscrutable.

"Which of these horses," said he to the gang on the fence-top, "would you take?"

"This one!" said an eager spokesman. "He didn't move a muscle since they hitched 'im."

This recommendation decided the matter instantly. Repose of manner is an estimable trait in the horse.

Geoffrey looked his animal over with an artist's eye. It was a slender creature, with that spare type of beauty that we associate with the Airedale dog. The horse was not a blond. The stirrups hung invitingly at the sides. Geoffrey closed the inspection with satisfaction, and prepared to mount.

In mounting, does one first untie one's horse and then get on, or may one, as in a steam-launch, get seated first and then cast off the painter? Geoffrey could not help recalling a page from "Pickwick Papers," where Mr. Winkle is climbing up the side of a tall horse at the Inn, and the 'ostler's boy whispers, "Blowed if the gen'l'man wasn't for getting up the wrong side." Well, what governs the right and wrong side of a horse? Douglas Fairbanks habitually avoids the dilemma by mounting from above — from the roof of a Mexican monastery, for instance, or the fire-escape of an apartment house. From these points he lands, perpendicularly. With this ideal in mind, Geoffrey stepped on from the fence, clamped his legs against the sides of the horse, and walked him out into the street.

When I say that he walked him out into the street, I use the English language as I have seen it used in books, but I think that it was an experienced rider who first used the idiom. Geoffrey says that he did not feel, at any time that afternoon, any sensation of walking his horse, or of doing anything else decisive with him. He walked, to be sure, dipping his head and rearing it, like a mechanical swan. But on a horse you miss the sensation of direct control that you have with a machine. With a machine, you press something, and if a positive reaction does not follow, you get out and fix something else. Not so with the horse. When you get upon him you cut yourself off from all accurately calculable connection with the world. He is, in the last analysis, an independent personality. His feet are on the ground, and yours are not.

We bow to literary convention, therefore, when we say that Geoffrey walked his horse.

Far ahead of him, he saw the khaki backs

of two of his friends who were also walking their horses. One by one they ambled up to the green and took places in the ranks. Geoffrey discovered that his horse would stand well if allowed to droop his long neck and close his eyes. Judged as a military figure, however, he was a disgrace to the army. If you drew up the reins to brace his head, he thought it a signal to start, and you had to take it all back, hastily. With the relaxed rein he collapsed again, his square head bent in silent prayer.

With the approach of the band, however, all this changed. He reared tentatively. Geoffrey discouraged that. Then he curled his body in an unlovely manner — an indescribable gesture, a sort of sidelong squirm in semi-circular formation. His rider straightened him out with a fatherly slap on the flank.

It was time to start. The band led off. Joy to the world, thought the horse, the band is gone. The rest of the cavalry moved forward in docile files, but not he. If that band was going away, he would be the last person to pursue it. Instead of going forward, he backed. He backed and backed. There is no emergency brake on a horse. He would have backed to the end of the procession, through the Knights of Columbus, the Red Cross, the Elks, the Masons, the D.A.R., the Fire Department, and the Salvation Army, if it had not been for the drum-corps that led the infantry. The drum-corps behind him was as terrifying as the band in front. To avoid the drum-corps, he had to spend part of his time going away from it. Thus his progress was a little on the principle of the pendulum. He backed from the band until he had to flee before the drums.

The ranks of men were demoralized by needless mirth. Army life dulls the sensibilities to the spectacle of suffering. They could do nothing to help, except to make a clear passage for Geoffrey as he alternately backed from the brasses and escaped from the drums. Vibrating in this way, he could only discourse to his horse with words of feigned affection, and pray for the panic to pass off. With a cranky automobile, now, one could have parked down a side street, and later joined the procession, all trouble repaired. But there was nothing organic the matter with this horse. Geoffrey could not have parked him in any case, because it would have been no more possible to turn him toward the cheering crowds on the pavement than to make him follow the band. The crowds on the street, in fact, began to regard these actions as a sort of interesting and decorative manœuvre, so regular was the advance and retirement — something in the line of a cotillion. And then the band stopped playing for a little. Instantly the horse took his place in the ranks, marched serenely, arched his slim neck, glanced about. All was as it should be.

Geoffrey's place was just behind the marshal, supposedly to act as his aide. During all this absence from his post of duty, the marshal had not noticed his defection or turned around at all. Now he did so, hastily.

"Just slip back, will you," he said, "and tell Monroe not to forget the orders at the reviewing stand."

Geoffrey opened his mouth to explain his disqualifications as courier, but at that moment the band struck up, and his charger backed precipitately. The marshal, seeing this prompt obedience to his request, faced front, and Geoffrey was left steadily receding, no time to explain — and the drum-corps was taking a vacation. There was, therefore, no reason for the horse ever to stop backing, unless he should back around the world until he heard the band behind him again. As he backed through the ranks of infantry, Geoffrey shouted the marshal's message to the officer of the day. He had to talk fast — ships that pass in the night. But the message was delivered, and he could put his whole mind on his horse.

He tried all the signals for forward loco-motion that he could devise. Mother had told him that some horses wait for light touches from their master's hand or foot. Geoffrey touched his animal here and there, back of the ear — at the base of the brain. He even kicked a trifle. He jerked the reins in Morse Code and Continental, to the tune of S O S. The horse understood no codes.

They were now in the ranks of the Knights of Columbus, and the marching boys were making room for them with shouts of sympathetic glee. Must they back through the Red Cross, where all the girls in town were marching, and into the Daughters of the Revolution float where our mother sat with a group of ladies around the spinning-wheel? Geoffrey remembered that the Red Cross had a band, if it would only play. It struck up just in time. The horse instantly became a fugitive in the right direction. On they sped, the reviewing stand almost in sight. The drum-corps had not begun to play. Could they reach the cavalry before it was too late? Geoffrey hated to pass the reviewing stand in the guise of a deserter, yet here he was cantering among the Odd Fellows, undoubtedly A.W.O.L.

But Heaven was kind. The drums waited. Through their ranks dashed Geoffrey at full speed, and into the midst of his companions. The reviewing stand was very near. At a signal, all bands and all drums struck up together. The horse, in stable equilibrium at last, daring not to run forward or to run backward, or to bolt to either side, fell into step and marched. Deafening cheers, flying handkerchiefs; Geoffrey and his horse stole past, held in the ranks by a delicate balance of four-cornered fear. If you fear something behind you and something in front of you, and things on both sides of you, and if your fear of all points of the compass is precisely equal, you move with the movements of the globe. Geoffrey's horse moved that way past the stand.

People took their pictures. Our father, beaming down from the galaxy on the stand, was pleased. Later he told Geoffrey how well he sat his horse.

But that evening Geoffrey had a talk with his mother, as man to man. He told her that, if these Victory Parades were going to be held often, he should vote for compulsory military training for the horse. He told her the various things his horse had done, how he went to and fro, going to when urged fro, and going fro when urged not to.

"Probably he had been trained to obey the opposite signals," said our mother. "You must study your horse as an individual."

That horse was an individual. Geoffrey studied him as such. He is quite willing to believe that he had been trained to obey the opposite signals. But Geoffrey says that he still cannot stifle one last question in his mind: — signals opposite to what?

BLIND FAITH

Some horses are products of fantasy, like Pegasus. Some become legends in fire, like Bucephalus. Some grow in the heart, like my own Great Day — and like this next horse, who was nothing less than miraculous.

His name was Blind Faith, and he belonged to Judy Bonham, a California trainer who acquired him in 1964 from someone who had spent money training him and then decided he didn't want to ride. Judy got the horse when he was three and took him to the Appaloosa shows, where she did so well that he was champion in the Appaloosa division in 1966 and 1968. She traveled all over, turned him into a champion reiner, and when he was thirteen years old he began having trouble with his eyes. They started watering a great deal, and a cloud formed on one eye. The vet said it was cataracts and that he would eventually lose his eyesight. His advice?

"Keep riding him."

Judy was surprised to hear that.

"He trusts you," the vet told her. "He'll go where you tell him. Just keep him in a box stall. As long as he knows his area, he'll be fine."

Judy knew when the horse had lost his sight because she'd put his food down and at first he couldn't find it. Then he learned, by scent, how, where, and when to locate it.

During this period, Judy continued to ride him. He acted as though he were sighted because he had formed such a bond with Judy that he trusted her to be his eyes. And not just by signals from the reins or her legs when she was riding. She recalls:

"When we traveled and I led him to the trailer, I'd go 'Step, step, step,' and he'd step his foot up and put it on the ramp and then walk on in."

So his cues were olfactory and auditory. And that's not all. When Judy took him to a show, he would measure the length he would have to run. He would somehow remember the number of strides it took or he'd recognize the different sound near the wall or possibly he'd notice the change in the air circulation, possibly all of the above — and he would know when to stop or turn or execute another reining maneuver.

"And I never cued him," Judy remembers. "Never once. He would slow down when we neared where he knew he would have to stop and I did the rest."

The trust was absolute. But soon, Judy realized, it became more than that. When she would put him in the trailer to travel, he would kick, or he would buck, or he would throw himself from side to side. But if she sat in the horse trailer with him, he would ride quietly. This big, powerful animal . . . this small, gentle human . . . in his mind, balance was restored.

When Judy finally decided to retire Blind Faith, in 1979, it was solely due to his age, not his blindness. He lived with Judy on her ranch. Throughout the early 1980s he suffered from almost chronic bronchial sickness and — I'll let Judy tell the rest.

"I just couldn't let him suffer, so I had him put down," she says tearfully.

"The vet came and I held him, and they just gave him the drugs to put him to sleep and he just went down and I just sat there with him and petted him until he was not there anymore. I wouldn't let the renderer come to take his body until after he was gone. It was heartbreaking but, you know, I looked at it this way: I said, 'I know I'll be riding him again someday.' He just did so much for me."

That is a fascinating, wonderful comment: *"He just did so much for me."* One might think, on the surface, that it was the other way around. Judy took care of him, never lost faith in Blind Faith despite his affliction, helped him to lead a very full life. Yet he did so much for her. Again, as she puts it:

"He made me who I am," she says. "My total empathy for animals, my outlook on them, and the fact that he made me grow and mature as a horse trainer. That was why I gave him the name I did: he had so much faith in me. I had a deeply spiritual connection with that horse and he just — I think there are certain horses that are so sensitive to you and your feelings that they become a part of you and your desires. Blind Faith was that horse."

"WHITE DANDY"; OR, MASTER AND I

BY VELMA CALDWELL MELVILLE (1898)

This novel, like the true-life tale of Blind Faith, is a fun and poignant story, and I offer up the first two chapters.

The selection has another value, one that makes stories written in any other era so important. I remember, growing up, reading novels like James Fenimore Cooper's *The Pioneers* or Mary Shelley's *Frankenstein.* Fiction is often a snapshot of the time when it was written, riddled with customs, habits, tools, and thoughts that are otherwise lost to us. There are props in this tale that evoke what it was like to own a horse well over a century ago. The language, too, is a reminder of another time, when a word like "bungler" was truly an invective. . . .

I suspect that the tale (and the title) were inspired by the success of an earlier novel by one Anna Sewell, the classic *Black Beauty* since *White Dandy* was billed as a companion piece.

CHAPTER I.

Master is Dr. Richard Wallace and I am Dandy, the doctor's favorite horse, long-tried companion and friend.

Neither of us are as young as we once were, but time seems to tell less on us than on some others, though I have never been quite the same since that dreadful year that Master was out West. He often strokes my face and says: "We're getting old, my boy, getting old, but it don't matter." Then I see a far away look in the kind, blue eyes — a look that I know so well — and I press my cheek against his, trying to comfort him. I know full well what he is thinking about, whether he mentions it right out or not.

Yes, I remember all about the tragedy that shaped both our lives, and how I have longed for intelligent speech that I might talk it all over with him.

He is sixty-two now and I only half as old, but while he is just as busy as ever, he will not permit me to undertake a single hardship.

Dr. Fred — his brother and partner — sometimes says: "Don't be a fool over that old horse, Dick! He is able to work as any of us." But the latter smiles and shakes his head: "Dandy has seen hard service enough and earned a peaceful old age."

Fred sneers. He says he has no patience with "Dick's nonsense;" but then he was in Europe when the tragedy occurred, and besides I suppose it takes the romance and sentiment out of a man to have two wives, raise three bad boys and bury one willful daughter, to say nothing of the grandson he has on his hands now; and I might add further that he is a vastly different man from Dick anyway. It is a grand thing to spend one's life for others; that is what my master has done, and it is what we horses do. Of course he is looking forward to his reward, but we are not expecting anything, though he insists that there will be a heaven for all faithful domestic animals. Fred says there is no Bible for it, but Dick says that they could not mention everything in one book. He says, too, that while he believes everything to be true that is in the Bible, at the same time he knows many things to be true that are not there; then he tells about a good old minister, who, when asked to lend his influence in the organization of a society for the prevention of cruelty to animals, replied that if Paul had written a chapter on the subject he would consider it worth his while to countenance the movement, but as he didn't, he must be excused.

For the benefit of such men, Master says he wishes the apostle had had time and inclination to write a chapter, and since he did not — with due reverence for Paul — it would have suited him better, and met a nineteenth century need closer, if he had omitted suggestions on ladies' toilets and dealt a few of his sledge-hammer blows at the man who oppresses the defenseless. Of course I know nothing about such things myself, but Dr. Dick has always had a fashion of talking all sorts of things to me, and I have a retentive memory.

But I must begin my story, for I have set out to give you a history of "Master and I" and, incidentally, of many another man and beast.

I will begin shortly after the tragedy; maybe before I get through I will tell you about that, but to-day I do not feel equal to it.

Poor Master!

Well, he came into my stall, where I had literally shivered with terror ever since that dreadful morning four days before, and, throwing his arms about my neck, burst into tears. A long while he sobbed there, and then growing calmer, he began caressing me, and said:

"Dandy, boy, you are going home with

me, to live with me while I live, to walk beside my coffin, and to be shot beside my grave, if so be you outlive me."

Sad words, but they were a comfort to me, feeling as I did.

Presently the boy came in and groomed me until my snowy coat shone like silk.

"I hate to part with ye, Dandy, fer fact I do!" he said, standing off and looking me over, "but then ye'd a gone anyhow, I s'pose." Then he put a halter on me and led me out to where the doctor's horses were standing hitched to a buggy and tied me fast to the back.

All the folks came out of the house and surely they cried harder than on either of those other days, but the doctor, with his lips white and set close together, hurried into the buggy and, with a backward nod, drove off. I glanced back and neighed good-by, then took up my journey with a heavy heart. I wanted to go and yet I wanted to stay. Certainly it was not enlivening to have to watch my master's agony all that weary seventy miles to his home.

Of course we stopped over night, and my first night it was away from home. I assure you that I felt lonely and wretched enough.

"Give all my horses the best of care," Master said to the hostler, "especially the white one."

The man promised and led us away.

"Don't s'pose they're any better'n other nags," he muttered, the minute we were out of hearing, and he took us to the pump, tired and heated as we were, and gave us all the water we could drink.

"What would Dr. Dick say?" Queen, one of the span of bays, said, as we turned away.

Of course the man did not understand, but thinking she was calling for more water he pumped another pailful and offered it to her. In surprise she turned her head aside, which so angered him, that he dashed the whole of the water right on to her.

Then he led us into dark, dirty stalls, roughly removed the harness from the bays and threw us some hay. When he was gone, at least we could not hear him, Queen said:

"I am all of a shiver; I believe it was the cold water inside and out. Dear me, I wish Master would come out."

"So do I," said Julie. "One thing is sure, we will have to stand up all night, I can never lie down in this filthy place."

"I don't think I could if I wanted to," responded Queen, "I am tied so short."

Meanwhile, I was nosing the hay, but it smelled so musty and something in it tickled my nostrils.

Presently I asked them if they could eat it.

"Oh, yes," Julie answered, "if you are going to be a doctor's horse you'll get worse than this."

Being pretty hungry, I nibbled away at it until a groan from Queen startled me. "Ain't you any better?" queried Julie. "No, I am shaking so I can hardly stand; how I do wish I had a blanket!"

"Wonder he don't see to rubbing us down," I said.

"Rubbing us down!" Julie spoke with scorn. "Unless Master comes out himself, as he generally does, there'll be no rubbing down to-night. About daylight they'll come around with an old currycomb and all but take the skin off us, along with the mud that will be formed out of the sweat and dust that ought to be rubbed off to-night."

"Oh, I wish Master would come!" moaned Queen; "I am almost burning up now."

"Got fever," remarked her mate, who seemed to have been around the world a good deal and grown used to everything.

After what seemed an age, a light flashed into the barn and two strange horses were tied in the next stalls. The same man led them. After throwing them some hay he came into my stall.

"Here, you fool, why don't you eat your

hay, not muss over it?" he cried angrily, pushing it together with one hand while with the other he dealt me a blow across the nose. It was the first blow that I had ever received, and it hurt me in more ways than one. Just then a boy came in with a peck measure of oats.

"There hain't none o' these critters tetched their hay hardly; 'nd their boss hez gone to bed sick, so I guess we'll 'conomize on the oats till mornin'."

"All right."

"Humph!" said Julie, but Queen groaned and I felt like it.

Before morning of that wretched night I lay down; I could not help it, I was so tired, hungry and sad.

Sure enough, by daylight (or lantern light in that windowless barn) the man and boy were at us with currycombs as if we had had no more feeling than barn doors. Then we each had a meager portion of oats. Julie and I ate ours readily enough, but poor Queen was too ill.

When the man noticed this he swore a little, then lengthened her halter strap and ordered the boy to scatter some straw over the filth in all our stalls.

By and by Master came out looking wan and haggard in the dim light. "Poor girl!"

he said, tenderly, running his fingers along the edge of Queen's jaw to the pulse.

"Mercy, Queenie, what a pulse — ninety!" Then he questioned the man as to his care of us, but never a word of truth he got in reply, but we could not tell.

"Lead her out into the daylight," Dr. Dick ordered, adding: "Haven't you a lot or yard where all my horses can be turned in for awhile?"

The man demurred, but Master soon brought the landlord and we were taken out into the sunlight. So busy was the former administering a dose of aconite to Queen that he did not at first notice me, but when he did an angry ejaculation escaped his lips as he pointed to my side. I was astonished, too, when I saw instead of my spotless coat, a great yellow stain.

"Is that the kind of beds you provide?" he cried, turning to the landlord.

"I am sure there seemed to be clean straw in the stalls," the latter replied, "I'll ask the man."

"No need," answered the doctor, curtly, "I am the one to blame for trusting any man to take care of these good servants who cannot speak for themselves."

It was almost noon before we started and then the bays walked every step of the way.

Just before leaving, the span of horses that came in after us the night before were brought out, one of them limping painfully.

The owner unconcernedly seated himself in his buggy and took up the lines.

The doctor spoke of the animal's lameness.

"Oh, that is nothing, Jerry is always lame when he first starts, and nearly all the rest of the time, for that matter," he added, as if it were a good joke.

"Why don't you have the trouble investigated?"

"Oh, I don't know; never thought much about it; he's an old horse," and with this he drove off.

Dr. Fred's first wife and her two boys were waiting to — but you can't understand what for yet. There were not so many railroads and lines of telegraph then, and no intimation of the news we brought had reached her. She cried and petted Dr. Dick as if he had been her own child. She put her arms about my neck and kissed me, too, making me think of other arms and other kisses. Ah me!

That Mrs. Fred was a lovely woman, more fit for Dr. Dick than his brother.

The Wallaces lived in the small country village of K —— and controlled a large practice. The brothers were ambitious, but had started poor, and not until the year before had they felt that either could spend a few months abroad. Fred was the elder, and there were other reasons why Dick preferred to go later, so it happened that the former was the last of the family for me to know.

The Wallace barn was a large frame building, warm in winter, cool, from having perfect ventilation, in summer, and well lighted.

Dr. Dick would have no hay mowed to be dropped into the mangers, nor would he have it stored directly above us all. He insisted that the dust would inevitably sift down and be the cause of various diseases of the eye, ear, throat and lungs.

He was particular about the stalls and feed boxes, too. He said it was a shame for an animal with a low body and short neck to be expected to take any comfort eating from a box put up for a high horse with a long neck. He had each stall fitted up with reference to its occupant, nor would he allow us to be put where we did not belong.

Queen and Julie were regular long, clean-limbed roadsters and their feed boxes were much higher than mine. I am of heavy build, with short legs and neck. The first time Dr. Fred looked me over — when Dr. Dick was absent — he remarked: "A pretty horse for a doctor! Slow and clumsy! No endurance!"

CHAPTER II.

Besides the bays, the Wallaces owned one other horse, old Ross, a somewhat worn and battered veteran, who entertained me for hours at a time, when we were standing alone in the shady pasture or in the barn, with tales of what he had seen, known and experienced.

"You look like a nice young fellow," he said on the second day of my arrival; "but I'd rather be myself, all battered up as I am, than you, for I have the satisfaction of knowing that I can't live many years longer and you may happen to suffer through a long lifetime yet."

"Why," I said, "is it so bad as that to live? I have always had a good time."

"Yes, it is very bad to live if you are owned by some people. Of course I am happy and contented here, only I know I shall be sold by and by. I am about worn out, and Dr. Fred said before he went away that I was getting too stiff for a doctor's horse."

"But my Master is never going to sell me!"

"How do you know that?"

"He says I am going to live with him always, and be shot beside his grave."

"Well, Dr. Dick is an exception among men; but he don't always get his way."

The season following my coming to K—— proved to be a never-to-be-forgotten one. Cholera raged for many weeks, and I had to take my share of the work, especially as Queen was not strong. She was never as well again before that night in the livery stable. She took cold easily and could not endure fatigue. Days and nights together Master never rested and scarcely ate anything, but in one sense it was a good thing; it helped him forget.

One day he had had the bays out since just after midnight and Ross had fallen terribly lame the day before, so when a call came for him to go a dozen or more miles in a pouring rain he was obliged to saddle me.

"Poor little Dandy!" he said, "your legs are too short for such a journey, but it is life or death to the mother of seven little ones."

That was enough for me; my legs might be short but they were strong, and though the doctor was heavy I felt equal to the task. I started off on a swift canter but Master drew rein, telling me to husband my strength for the last half of the way.

It had long been dark when we arrived — inky dark, too, with no cessation of the rainfall. A trembling hand held out a lantern while a hollow voice fairly sobbed: "I'm afeard ye're too late, doctor, my woman is sinking fast."

"Now, see here, my man, you take good care of my noble little horse here and I'll pull the wife through, or fail doing my best."

By the uncertain light of the lantern I saw that I was being tied in a sort of shed. My saddle was removed, but its place was soon supplied by a stream of water that trickled through a hole in the roof. Move which way I would, a leak was directly over my back. The man laid some newly-cut grass across some poles, barely within my reach, and went away.

All the while I was aware that the place had another occupant, though I could see nothing. Presently a horse's voice in the darkness asked if I had come far. From the first tone I noticed a sadness, but I replied to the question, adding that I would rather be out of doors than in this leaky place.

"Oh," she said, "this ain't bad now, but it is a dreary place in winter with the snow drifting in and the wind whistling through."

I was too much surprised to answer at

first, and in a minute she gave a long, piteous whinny.

"Whom are you calling?" I asked.

"My baby, my pretty, little roan colt; they took him from me last week and have not brought him back. It seems as if my heart must break! We were never separated an hour before, and I don't see how he will get along alone. My baby, oh, my baby!"

I expressed my pity for her, and she said it did her good to have some one to talk to.

"Oh, it is a dreadful thing to be a mother, loving your offspring as much as human mothers do, and yet be speechless and helpless," she moaned.

"They tied me in here and drove Selim into a corner and caught him. I jerked and neighed until master kicked me and bade me shut my head. By this time the others had got Selim out, and I could hear him calling to me. His voice grew fainter and fainter and then all was still."

"I suppose your master sold him. Ross, the old horse at our place, says he was taken from his mother and sold."

"Oh me! if colts must be taken from their mothers in that way, why can't they get us used to the separation by degrees, not tear us apart without a moment's warning or word of farewell?"

"Why can't they?" I repeated, then added: "But I guess your master is getting pay now for his cruelty. His wife is almost dying with cholera, and my master says there are seven little children."

"I shall certainly pity the children if they are deprived of a mother's care, but they will feel no worse than little Selim does."

After a while Dr. Dick came out to the shed. I suppose the rain had ceased by that time, at least the stream of water on my back had, but I was standing in some sort of filth, with the mud hardening on my legs. A long while he scraped and rubbed my legs and back, then turned me out into a little pasture.

"It will be better than this dirty place, Dandy," he said, and it was.

It was just growing gray in the morning when a man rode past the pasture on a horse that fairly swayed from side to side, he was so exhausted, and blood and foam poured from his mouth and nostrils.

In a minute more Dr. Dick was calling me.

"Likely you'll have a time to ketch the colt," the owner of the premises was saying as I came up. The doctor laughed.

"Why, that is queer," the man said. "I can never get near the old mare, even when she's out."

"Well, sir," replied Master, looking very serious, "I would be ashamed to treat a dumb animal so badly that it would fear to come at my call. My horses know that I am their friend, and that, though I may have to work them hard, I will not require more of them than they can do, and that they can trust me in all things."

Then he stroked my face, and I put my cheek against his.

"Dandy and I love each other," he added. Then he went for the saddle and bridle. My companion of the evening before was still neighing pitifully, and Master inquired the cause.

"Sir, if your wife or any of your children die," he said severely, when the other had told about the colt, "just remember that you deserve it, for having no regard for the feelings of a dumb mother. The God who noteth the sparrow's fall, will measure unto you as you measure unto the helpless. There is a merciful and humane way of dealing in all these matters. If I were in your place, I'd send one of the boys to bring that colt where its mother can see it for a day and then let her watch it go away. 'Blessed are the merciful, for they shall obtain mercy.' "

We now joined the other man standing

beside his heaving horse at the gate.

"Follow at your leisure; that poor beast is well-nigh done for; I will hurry on and do all I can," Dr. Dick said to the stranger, whose sister had been attacked by the epidemic; and away we flew.

My training had all been for the saddle, and, whether built right or not, I was at home under it. We turned in at the Wallace gateway just forty-eight hours after going out of it.

"How did the colt stand it?" was the hired man's first query.

"Dandy is a jewel, Bob!" Master replied heartily, "a perfect saddle horse and with ambition and sense enough for a dozen horses."

And thus began my actual experience as a doctor's horse; and from that time on our names were continually associated together, first by the family and finally by the whole town and neighborhood.

I remember one small boy, coming in haste for the doctor, breathlessly announced that he had come for "Dick and Dandy."

I was soon trained to drive in a sulky, and grew to like it better than the saddle, only that I could not hear quite as well what the doctor said to me — in common conversation — as we traveled along.

The news of the epidemic brought Dr. Fred home some little time before he intended coming, but his coming brought no additional happiness to the stables, whether it did to the house or not.

He rushed about everything, spoke in a loud, confusing tone, issued one order only to countermand it by another, used profane language and — drank whisky.

"We've had our good time," Ross remarked significantly, and Julie gave an acquiescent snort.

Meanwhile a new blacksmith had bought out the old one in K—— and Dr. Dick was wondering if the former was a bungler. Ross did not get over his lameness, and Master had had his shoes removed and turned him out into the pasture.

THE STABLE AS CATHEDRAL

For most people — perhaps all? — wherever they love to be, that place is a cathedral to them. A place of solemn joy, perhaps a place of great spiritual portent. For athletes it might be a stadium — empty or filled, it doesn't matter. Perhaps it's a hilltop under the vault of the sky. For many actors, it's a stage.

For me, it's a stable.

I do love the stage, any stage, but I go there to work. I love my work, but that's not the same as my love of riding . . . and stables.

Let me tell you a little bit about the place where I feel most spiritual. Before I do that, keep in mind that I have been to truly sacred and highly spiritual places. I've been in sweat lodges, I've been in smoke ceremonies where a shaman drifts smoke over you, I've been at the confluence of several mountains near Mount Everest where there was a great Buddhist temple, where all the spirits were supposed to flow. It was beautiful, it was incredibly serene, it was filled with the energy of ages gone by. But what I got from that was not a *spiritual* experience. I understand where others could find those places profoundly spiritual. For me, something personally relatable must be present. I could be talking to any one of you and have a spiritual experience. I could be in front of a camera, working with an inspirational actor.

Or I could be in a stable.

I am not entirely sure if one picture could replace these thousand or so words. When there are horses present, when I first enter it is a sort of idyllic passage, if you will. Something happens to me. You enter and you stand in the semi-darkened light and the first thing you smell is the sweet/sour odor of horses mixed with the nose-alerting scent of manure. There are all kinds of perfumes in each balloon of air, including the smell of the leather, the smell of the leather oil. For me that unique mixture is almost like a pheromone. It triggers a social response. I begin to feel closer to the animals than I do to my own species.

There's dust in the air. The light filters in through the particles that come from all the hay, and the feed, and the horses' hair.

These motes hang suspended, weightless in the columns of light. They stir as you pass, or if the stable is airy they are constantly drifting in lazy, unpredictable ways.

Then there's the sight of the horses themselves, especially the eyes, which are beacons. And in those eyes you can see many things: the dreamy state of some of the horses, the angry state, the anxious eyes imploring, "When do I get out? When do I eat?" There are many kinds of emotions hiding in the stalls but, over all, in a well-run barn, there is a feeling of peacefulness, and contentment.

There are sounds, too. The slap of the leather when saddles are moved. There's the ever-present crunch of the hay, like background music. There's the staccato rumble, like timpani, of the poured corn and mash that has grain in it, a mix so sweet that the horses hunger for it because it's like candy. They whinny for it, over it. And of course, there is the occasional drumbeat of horse hooves. There are also the subtler shuffles of the horses' inner rhythms. They never quite stand still, they're always shifting their weight from one leg to another. Or there's the impatient stamp of a horse anxious to get out, or anticipating eating, or anticipating riding. There are the soloist sounds of dog barks. There's a symphony of orchestration in a barn, and if you just tune in, it becomes massive and melodic.

I mentioned the dogs. Wherever the stable, in whatever part of the world, you and the horses are never alone. Dogs are always part of the stable. The Jack Russells hunt mice and rats. Sometimes they'll lay them at your feet, proudly. The longer, leaner dogs accompany you on the ride.

There are birds. Not only are there birds but there are birds' nests, because they eat the seeds that fall along every avenue from a horse. Eventually, they just make their home at the source.

The animals serve a dual purpose, though. Since horses are herd animals, those horses that leave the comfort of their own stall with some frequency, or who are competitive and are inclined to make trouble with other horses — these animals will be given a friend that they come to view as a noncompetitive member of their herd. I've heard of chickens, I've heard of goats, I've heard of pigs, I've heard of dogs, I've heard of cats. All have been substitute herd members and the horse would be very uncomfortable if they were shipped without their friend.

Naturally, the rider isn't the only human in a stable. There are a variety of people who visit stalls on a regular basis, stables on a regular basis. And these people add to the mix as well. There's the trainer, who is the boss, who says this horse needs that, and that horse needs this. There are the stable boys and girls, whose daily work is to feed and curry the horses. There are the owners, who come at prescribed times to visit with their horses and perhaps learn from their horses, and ride their horses. There is the occasional visitor who has been mesmerized by horses and just wants to pet them and be part of the experience.

There are children, too.

For the most part, horses want to befriend humans of all kinds — but they seem to acknowledge that a smaller, weaker person requires something of a change in behavior toward them. And they quite frequently are more gentle, more giving. I've seen that among my horses often.

Conversely, every so often there is a dangerous air from a stranger, whose association with horses is suspect, and everybody keeps an eye on that dark cloud of an individual, who may or may not be there for nefarious purposes, but gives off that vibe. Like a dog with its hair up, everybody reacts to that person and protects the horses. In a stable, the horse is everyone's top priority.

With all of these elements active and in play, there is also rich, ripe expectation, the anticipation of mounting the horse and being part of the horse, and having a period of union with the horse in the outdoors.

I have come to realize that with any spiritual place, there are two major components: the energy that you bring and the energy that is brought, and left there, by others. Does the memory of a "big game" ever truly leave a stadium? Does the emotion of a wedding or a funeral ever leave a church or temple?

A stable has all of those energies, the triumphs and joys and sadness. And there are two more reasons it is like a cathedral. First, being there has made me a better person and a better actor. Being one with a horse has made me understand, even better, being one with a role, letting the dialogue and the character emerge from an inner place and not being afraid of what comes with it.

The second reason is perhaps the most important of all. When you enter a cathedral, you take off your hat and bow your knee. You embrace humility.

If you are lucky, that, above all, stays with you.

A RACE HORSE THAT PAID A CHURCH DEBT

Taking Chances,
BY CLARENCE LOUIS CULLEN (1900)

Mr. Cullen authored all kinds of stories for *The New York Sun* — including many about games of chance — which were collected in *Taking Chances.* He wrote amusingly in the introduction:

To the man who, at any period of his days, has been bitten by that ferocious and fever-producing insect colloquially known as the "horse bug," and likewise to the man whose nervous system has been racked by the depredations of the "poker microbe," these tales of the turf and of the green cloth are sympathetically dedicated. The thoroughbred running horse is a peculiar animal. While he is often beaten, the very wisest veterans of the turf have a favorite maxim to the effect that "The ponies can't be beat" — meaning the thoroughbred racers; which sounds paradoxical enough. Poker, too, is a mystifying affair, in that all men who play it appear, from their own statements, to lose at it persistently and perennially. There is surely something weird and uncanny about a game that numbers only losers among its devotees.

"A friend of mine who came here from Chicago for the Bennings meeting was telling me about that Jim McCleevy mule," said an old-time owner of thoroughbreds who is wintering a string of jumpers and breaking a bunch of yearlings out at the Bennings track. "That makes a queer story, and there are some strange things connected with the thoroughbred game, at that. This McCleevy horse wasn't worth a bag of moist peanuts at the beginning of the present racing season. He couldn't beat a fat man. He had never been in the money. He was a legitimate thousand-to-one shot in any company. He was the candidate for the shafts of a brick cart, when by some odd chance he passed into the possession of a nice young woman who was going to school somewhere in the State of Iowa. The girl's uncle was mixed up some way or another with the turf, and he bought the McCleevy plug for a joke, paying a few dollars for him. In a spirit of fun he wrote to his niece that he had bought Jim McCleevy in her name, and that the horse belonged to her and would be run in her interest. The young woman didn't know the difference between a race-horse and a chatelaine bag. She was an orphan, and struggling to get an education for herself. Her ambition was to take a course at a woman's college, but, up to the time of this incident, which lasted throughout the spring and summer, her hope of putting this ambition over the plate was pretty shadowy, and it looked like it was up to her to get a job teaching at a country school in order to support herself. But she wrote to her uncle that she accepted the gift of the no-account racer with gratitude, and inquired if the horse could not trot right fast, for, if so, she might be able to dispose of him to some well-to-do farmer in her neighborhood.

"Jim McCleevy was attached to the string of a good trainer, who saw at once that the horse had been underestimated, that he had been badly handled, and that it would be worth the effort to try to make something of him. He spent two or three weeks monkeying with the skate and fixing him up, and then he sent him out one morning with a lummux of a stable boy on his back and put the watch on him. Jim McCleevy breezed a mile in 1:44, fighting for his head at the finish, and two days later he was slapped into a selling race at a mile and a sixteenth, with light weight, a bum apprentice lad up, and all kinds of a price, for there were some good ones in the race, which was at the Harlem track, in Chicago. The girl's uncle scattered a few dollars around the ring on the mutt, all three ways, and McCleevy came home on the bit. That was the beginning of McCleevy. He was put into a couple of races a week at a mile and more, at the Harlem and Hawthorne tracks, during the entire racing season at Chicago, and he won race after race, no matter how they piled the weight penalties up on him. When he didn't win he broke into the money, and as there was always a good price on him, seeing that almost every time he raced he was pitted against horses that seemed to outclass him, the uncle of the girl who owned him got some of the money every time. He parleyed the money that he won for his niece on Jim McCleevy's first race, and he got it back and a bunch besides every time. The fame of Jim McCleevy spread around Chicago, and a Chicago newspaper man went down to Iowa to interview the young woman who owned the horse. She told him, artlessly, that while she abhorred gambling — well, she certainly did enjoy the prospect of being enabled to complete her education.

Her uncle deposited between $8,000 and $9,000 in her name, the amount he had won for her in purses and bets on Jim Mc-Cleevy, at the wind-up of the racing season, and the horse, which developed quite a bit of real class, still belongs to her.

"Odd, isn't it, that an underestimated race-horse should hop out and not only give a nice girl that had never so much as has stroked his sleek neck a chance to fulfill her ambition for an education, but win her a start in life that'll probably make her one of the eligible girls in the State of Iowa? But I recall a queerer one than that — how a cast-off crab suddenly developed into a race-horse and paid off a mortgage on a church.

"That happened out at Latonia four years ago. I was racing a few of my own out there at the time, and saw the affair from the beginning to the wind-up. I'll have to duck giving the names, for the good man who profited by the sudden development of the nag he accidentally became possessed of is still the pastor of a flock that congregates in a pretty little debt-free, brick and stone Roman Catholic church on the outskirts of Cincinnati.

"There was an old trainer hanging around the Latonia barns at that time who was in hard luck from a whole lot of different points of view. I'd known him on the metropolitan tracks years before, and he had been, in his day of prosperity, a good fellow and a horse-wise man, if ever one chewed a straw. When his health went back on him, however, six or seven years ago, and he couldn't personally attend to his work — he ran an open training stable — it was all off with him. The strings that he had been handling were taken away from him by the owners and put in other hands, and he went up against the day of adversity with a rattle. He had a few horses of his own, but these proved worthless, and most of them were finally taken away from him to pay feed bills. On top of it all he developed locomotor ataxia, and when I got out to the Latonia barns, four years ago, he could barely move around. How he contrived to exist I don't know, but I guess the boys chipped in a dollar or so every once in a while for the old man. The only horse that he had left when I reached Latonia with my little bunch was an old six-year-old gelding that was a joke. Well, call him Caspar. The mention of Caspar's name made even the stable-boy grin. Caspar looked a good deal like Diggs, that camel horse that's pulling down the purses now in New Orleans. He was all out of shape, with a pair of knees on him each as big as your hat; of all the bunged up, soured, chalky old skates that ever I looked over, this Caspar gelding was the limit. Yet he had been a pretty good two-year-old and a more than fair three-year-old. He had won four races as a two-year-old, and six as a three-year-old, but he was campaigned and drummed a heap, and when the old man shot him as a four-year-old Caspar could just walk, and that's all. He was a cripple from every point of the compass. He was chronically sour and sore, and he was as vicious and ugly as the devil, into the bargain. He never got anywhere near the money as a four and five-year-old, and he hadn't been raced at all as a six-year-old, when I first clapped an eye on his rheumatic old shape. But the old man was a sentimentalist in his way, and he couldn't stand the idea of selling a horse that he had taken care of as a baby to some truck driver to be overworked and abused. So he hung on to Caspar, fed him, nursed him and took care of him generally, just as if the old plug was making good for all of this attention. Caspar was a standing gag around the Latonia stables.

" 'Wait'll I joggle Caspar under the string by four lengths in the Kentucky Derby!' a monkey-faced apprentice jockey would say solemnly to the other kids, and then they'd all holler.

"Well, about a month after I struck Latonia — it was then getting on toward midsummer — the old trainer in hard luck who owned Caspar took to his bunk, not to get up any more. He only lasted two weeks. Two days before he died he sent for an old Irish priest that he had known for a number of years. The priest was the pastor of that little brick and stone church on the outskirts of Cincinnati that I spoke about. The old trainer had been a good Catholic all his life, and he received the last offices of his faith. Then he said to the priest:

" 'Father, there's a crabbed, battered-up old dog of mine over at Latonia that I'll make you a present of. He's worth about one dollar and eighty cents, but he was a good racing tool when he was young, and I've never felt like turning him loose to hustle for himself. He's crippled up some, but you might get him broken to harness, so that he could haul your buggy around. I wish you'd take him and see that he doesn't get the worst of it. Caspar was pretty good to me a few times when I was up against it.'

"When the old man turns up his toes and dies the kindly priest came over to the barns to see if he could get any assistance in the way of putting our old hard-luck pal under the ground. He got it, of course, and enough for a tombstone besides. While he was at the stables the father thought he might as well have a look at the piece of horse-flesh that had been presented to him by the old man. So one of the trainers escorted him to Caspar's stall.

" 'Could he ever be made any good for driving purposes?' the priest asked the trainer, who smiled.

" 'He'd kick a piano-mover's truck into matchwood the first clatter out of the box,' replied the trainer.

" 'I'll just let him stay over here for awhile until I decide what to do with him,' said the priest, and he went back to Cincinnati and buried the old trainer.

"Well, a couple of mornings later a fresh stable-boy who had just got a job in one of the barns put a bridle and saddle on old Caspar and took him for a breeze around the course just for fun. It was just at dawn, and a lot of us trainers were watching the early morning work of the horses. It struck me when Caspar passed by the rail where I was standing that the old devil looked mighty skittish, and was doing a lot of prancing for a hammered-to-death skate, with bum knees and all sorts of other complaints. About a minute later there was

238

a yawp all along the rail.

" 'Get next to that old Caspar!' a lot of the trainers shouted. I looked over toward the back-stretch, and there was the old skate with his head down, eating up the ground like a racehorse. We all jerked out our watches just as he flashed by the five-furlong pole and put them on him. It was amazing to see the old mutt make the turn and come a-tearing down the stretch. If he didn't do that five furlongs in 1:02, darn me. All of our watches told the same story, and there was no mistake about it. When he passed the judges' stand Caspar wanted to go right ahead and work himself out, but we all hollered at the boy to pull him up. The kid stopped the old gelding with difficulty. Caspar wanted to run, and he had a mouth on him as hard as nails.

"We got together and talked about Caspar. We were dumbfounded, and didn't know what to make of that exhibition of speed. Then a trainer who was, and still is, noted throughout the country as the most skilful horse-patcher that ever got into the game spoke up.

" 'The old devil's just come back to himself, that's all there is about it,' he said. 'There are a lot of sprints in his old carcass yet. All he needs is some patching. If he'll run like this work he's just done in five-furlong dashes, there's a chance for a slaughter with him. I'm going to ask the father to let me handle him and see if he can't be oiled up.'

"The trainer went over to Cincinnati that same morning and saw the priest.

" 'Father,' said he, 'I don't want to get a man of your cloth mixed up with the racing game, but I think I can do something with that old racing tool, the old man bequeathed to you.' Then he told the priest about Caspar's phenomenal work that morning.

" 'Bless me!' said the good man, 'I fear it would not be seemly for me to' ——

" 'Oh, that end of it'll be all right, father,' said the trainer. 'If I find I can do anything with the old rogue I'll shoot him into a dash under my own colors, and you won't be entangled with the thing a little bit. It won't cost you anything to let me try him out, and if I find that he'll do I'll get my end of it by putting down — er — uh — well. I won't lose anything anyhow.'

"Well, when he left the kindly man of the cloth he had the permission to see what could be done with old Caspar. 'Let me know how you progress,' the priest had asked him.

"The trainer seeing a chance to make a

killing — and we all vowed ourselves to secrecy about the matter — went to old Caspar. He was a nag-patcher, as I say, from the foothills, and the way he applied himself to the reduction of Caspar's inflammations, and to the tonicking up in general of the old beast, was a caution to grasshoppers. And it came about that early morning's work of Caspar's that had surprised us so was no flash in the pan at all. The old 'possum had somehow or another recovered his speed all of a sudden, in addition to a willingness to run, in spite of his infirmities. At the end of two weeks Caspar, as fine a bit of patched-work as you ever saw, was ready. The trainer went over to Cincinnati and told the father so.

" 'Well,' inquired the priest.

" 'He's going to run in a five-furlong dash day after tomorrow,' said the trainer. 'And he'll walk. It is a copper-riveted cinch — er-uh — I mean, that is, Caspar will win, you see. It'll be write your own ticket, too. Any price. In fact when the gang sees his name among the entries, they'll think it's a joke.'

" 'My son,' said the father, with a certain twinkle lurking in the corner of his eye, 'gaming is a demoralizing passion. Nevertheless, if this animal, that came into my possession by such odd chance, possesses sufficient speed to — er' ——

" 'Oh, that's all right, father,' said the trainer and he bolted for it.

"As the trainer had said to the priest, there was an all-around chuckle the following afternoon when the entry sheets were distributed and it was seen that Caspar was in the five-furlong dash the next day. For a wonder, not a word had got out about the patching job that had been in progress on the old horse, nor about his remarkable work. The stable lads and railbirds who were on kept their heads closed and saved their nickels for the day of Caspar's victory.

"Well, to curl this up some, the field that we confidently expected Caspar to beat was made up of nine rattling good sprinters — one of them was so good that his price opened and closed at 4 to 5 on. Caspar was the rank outsider at 150 to 1. We all got on at that figure, the bookies giving us the laugh at first, and only a few of them wise enough to rub when they suspected that there was something doing. The trainers', railbirds', and stable-boys' money that went in forced the old skate's price down to 75 to 1 at post time. A number of us took small chunks of 100 to 1 in the poolrooms in Cincinnati — wired our commissions over.

The old horse favored his left forefoot a trifle in walking around to the starting pole, and that worried us a bit, for he'd been all right on his pin the night before. We didn't do any hedging, however, but stood by to see what was going to happen. All of us, of course, had enough down on him to finish third to pull us out in case he couldn't get the big end of the money.

"It was a romp for Caspar. If I'd tell you the real name of the horse you'd remember the race well. Caspar, with a perfect incompetent of a jockey on his back, jumped off in the lead, and was never headed, winning, pulled double and to a walk, by three lengths. The bookies made all colors of a howl over it, but their howls didn't go. They had to cough. It was the biggest killing that bunch of Latonia trainers, including myself, had ever made, and there wasn't a stable boy on the grounds that didn't have money to cremate for months afterward.

"After the race the trainer who had patched old Caspar up for the hogslaughtering — he was close on to $15,000 to the good, and he didn't have me skinned any, at that — hustled over to the priest's house.

" 'Father, the plug made monkeys of 'em,' is the way he announced Caspar's victory.

" 'Truly?' said the priest.

" 'Monkeys,' repeated the trainer, and then he pulled out a huge new wallet that he had bought on the way to the priest's residence. He handed the wallet to the father. 'When I was here, a couple o' days ago,' said the trainer, looking interestedly out of the window, 'I had along with me a fifty-dollar bill that, feeling pretty prosperous that morning, I intended to hand to you to be distributed among the poor of the parish — used to be an acolyte and serve mass myself, a good many years ago, when I was a kid. Well, I forgot to pass you the fifty, you see, and so I invested it in — er-uh — a little matter of speculation, to your account, so that it amounts to — er-uh — well, I understood there's a bit of a mortgage on your church, you know."

"The priest opened the wallet and counted out seven one thousands, one five hundred and one fifty-dollar bill. The trainer had put the $50 down on Caspar for the priest — without the father's sanction or countenance, of course — at 150 to 1.

" 'Well,' went on the trainer, anxious to talk so as to save any questions as to the nature of his speculation, 'it certainly would have done your heart good if you could have seen that old nag cantering down the stretch' ——

244

" 'It did,' said the father, with a smile. 'It is no sin, I conceive, for even a man of my cloth to watch noble beasts battling for the supremacy, there being, I take it, nothing cruel in such contests. I saw the race.'

"Old Caspar was wound up by that race. He went to the paddock as sore as a boil, all of his old infirmities breaking out with renewed strength, and he was turned out to grass and died comfortably two years ago. If he could have known, it might have cheered his declining days to realize that he had paid off the mortgage on a nice little brick and stone edifice of worship on the outskirts of Cincinnati."

The Reign of the Reining Horse

If the stable is a cathedral, reining is my prayer book.

I don't say that with any disrespect. To the contrary: it shows the considerable reverence I have for both.

Reining incorporates so many of the things I've spoken about. In a way, you can reverse-engineer my education: a lot of what I've learned, a lot of what I've been able to retrofit in my understanding of horses and horsemanship, comes from this sport.

A reining horse is trained to execute extraordinary bursts of energy, of galloping and sliding, for example, and then to stand absolutely still. That stillness is part of the equestrian skill. In that state, the horse meditates for an instant and then whirls into action for another completion of a move, and then stops and is still.

The ability to achieve this, with a horse, has been instilled in me in all these years of training. I have learned that in reining, as in life, periods of stillness and reflection are essential. In the sport, it becomes rhythmic expression at its best. This is not unique to reining — as we'll be discussing later in other disciplines such as martial arts, in that instant when Annie Oakley jumps a fence and shoots, in baseball during that heartbeat when batter and pitcher size one another up just before the pitch.

In that stillness you become totally aware, and then you ease into the next move using that pause, using that instant where the energy was trapped, tapped, and then released.

I can guarantee you that this was part of the training, part of the martial movements of horses in war. They would explode into motion at both ends, the front and back, kicking out, laying waste to the soldiers in front of them, and then coming to a stillness while the rider used his sword, and then doing the same thing again.

You see it in ancient art, certainly in the terra-cotta Chinese statues I will be discussing later: the utter stillness of the horses. They were caught in a moment at rest, as they paid obeisance to the emperor. But there was also inherent in those statues the ability to explode into action in a moment.

We talked about mythology earlier, but it's relevant to mention another figure here. I once saw an illustration of a horse in Norse mythology, Sleipnir, who was eight-legged. Add the two long legs of the rider and you have a lot of latent power. Was that an attempt by the Norse, in their own art, to depict motion? Or was it dramatic license to instill awe and fear of the courage and fortitude of the Norse riders?

Possibly both, but the feeling I got was of omniscient power. Eight legs: that's something you can't stop. It's something that's overwhelming. From what I have read, there is some connection between this depiction of Sleipnir and an effort among the Norse to embody the forces of elemental energy.

The technique of using the reins varies from rider to rider. Some trainers will be very harsh with their hands, jerking on that bit to keep the horse's head down, or level, or up, depending on what the horse is doing. Others prescribe a very gentle touch, and I've had those trainers explain it as, "Think of it as if that bit were in your mouth." So you very gently waddle that bit, saw back and forth with a delicate touch.

In either case, the reins are invaluable: they guide the horse left to right, are part of the accelerator and certainly part of the brakes.

The next important part of guiding a horse is your legs. The rider's leg on a horse is of equal importance to anything else. The horse is taught to move from the pressure of the leg. And after a while the horse becomes so sensitized that it's a lover's touch of your knee or your calf or your heel, depending on the severity of what you're doing. A feather's brush is all you'll need to guide the horse, because his sides have become so sensitive to your legs.

The third thing is your voice. You communicate with the horse by the way you cant, by the cluck, by the whoa, and everything in between. These help to accelerate and to brake the horse.

Acquainting the horse with these skills is what anyone must do if they want to become serious equestrians.

I love reining and I've been doing it for many years. But as with any sport, part of the joy is revisiting it day after day to see what new skills you can pick up.

I have a good friend, a martial artist, who says, "It takes a master to recognize how much more there is to learn."

ONLY THE MARE

BY ALFRED E. T. WATSON IN
*Sporting Society; or, Sporting Chat
and Sporting Memories, Vol. 1,*
EDITED BY FOX RUSSELL (1897)

Mr. Russell himself wrote prolifically about horses. He explained why in his volume *Cross Country Reminiscences:* "Pleasant it is for a man whose hand has oftener grasped a hunting crop than a pen, to sit down and try to put a few notes on paper, of some of the good things he has had the luck to participate in, and indulge in some homely-printed chat — to coin an expression — of good horses and good men."

When one opens a suspicious-looking envelope and finds something about "Mr Shopley's respectful compliments" on the inside of the flap, the chances are that Mr Shopley is hungering for what we have Ovid's authority for terming *irritamenta malorum.* Not wishing to have my appetite for breakfast spoiled, I did not pursue my researches into a communication of this sort which was amongst my letters on a certain morning in November; but turned over the pile until the familiar caligraphy of Bertie Peyton caught my eye: for Bertie was Nellie's brother, and Nellie Peyton, it had been decided, would shortly cease to be Nellie Peyton; a transformation for which I was the person chiefly responsible. Bertie's communication was therefore seized with avidity. It ran as follows: —

"The Lodge, Holmesdale.

"My dear Charlie,
    "I sincerely hope that you have no important engagements just at present, as I want you down here most particularly.
    "You know that there was a small race-meeting at Bibury the other day. I rode over on Little Lady, and found a lot of the 14th Dragoons there; that conceited young person Blankney amongst the number. Now, although Blankley has a very considerable personal knowledge of the habits and manners of the ass, he doesn't know much about the horse; and for that reason he saw fit to read us a lecture on breeding and training, pointing his moral and adorning his tale with a reference to my mare — whose pedigree, you know, is above suspicion. After,

however, he had kindly informed us what a thoroughbred horse ought to be, he looked at Little Lady and said, 'Now I shouldn't think that thing was thoroughbred!' It ended by my matching her against that great raw-boned chestnut of his: three and a half miles over the steeplechase course, to be run at the Holmesdale Meeting, on the 5th December.

"As you may guess, I didn't want to win or lose a lot of money, and when he asked what the match should be for, I suggested '£20 a-side.' 'Hardly worth while making a fuss for £20!' he said, rather sneeringly. '£120, if you like!' I answered, rather angrily, hardly meaning what I said; but he pounced on the offer. Of course I couldn't retract, and so very stupidly, I plunged deeper into the mire, and made several bets with the fellows who were round us. They laid me 3 to 1 against the mare, but I stand to lose nearly £500.

"You see now what I want. I ride quite 12 stone, as you know; the mare is to carry 11 stone, and you can just manage that nicely. I know you'll come if you can, and if you telegraph I'll meet you.

"Your's ever,
Bertie Peyton.
"P.S. — Nellie sends love, and hopes to see you soon. No one is here, but the aunt is coming shortly."

I was naturally anxious to oblige him, and luckily had nothing to keep me in town; so that afternoon saw me rapidly speeding southwards, and the evening, comfortably domiciled at The Lodge.

Bertie, who resided there with his sister, was not a rich man. £500 was a good deal more than he could afford to lose, and poor little Nellie was in a great flutter of anxiety and excitement in consequence of her brother's rashness. As for the mare, she could gallop and jump; and though we had no means of ascertaining the abilities of Blankney's chestnut, we had sufficient faith in our Little Lady to enable us to "come up to the scratch smiling;" and great hopes that we should be enabled to laugh at the result in strict accordance with the permission given in the old adage, "Let those laugh who win."

It was not very pleasant to rise at an abnormal hour every morning, and arrayed in great-coats and comforters sufficient for six people, to rush rapidly about the country; but it was necessary. I was a little too heavy, and we could not afford to throw away any weight, nor did I wish to have my saddle reduced to the size of a cheese-plate, as would have been my fate had I been unable to reduce myself. Breakfast, presided over by Nellie, compensated for all matutinal discomforts; and then she came round to the stables to give the mare an encouraging pat and a few words of advice and endearment which I verily believe the gallant little mare understood, for it rubbed its nose against her shoulder as though it would say, "Just you leave it in my hands — or, rather, to my feet — and I'll make it all right!" Then we started for our gallop, Bertie riding a steady old iron-grey hunter.

The fourth of December arrived, and the mare's condition was splendid. "As fit as a fiddle," was the verdict of Smithers, a veterinary surgeon who had done a good deal of training in his time, and who superintended our champion's preparation; and though we were ignorant of the precise degree of fitness to which fiddles usually attain, he seemed pleased, and so, consequently, were we. Unfortunately on this morning Bertie's old hunter proved to be very lame, so I was forced to take my last gallop by myself; and with visions of success on the morrow, I passed rapidly through the keen air over the now familiar way; for the course was within a couple of miles of the house, and so we had the great advantage of being able to accustom the mare to the very journey she would have to take.

Bertie was in a field at the back of the stables when I neared home again. "Come on!" he shouted, pointing to a nasty hog-backed stile, which separated us. I gave Little Lady her head, and she cantered up to it, lighting on the other side like a very bird! Bertie didn't speak as I trotted up to him, but he looked up into my face with a triumphant smile more eloquent than words.

"You've given her enough, haven't you?" he remarked, patting her neck, as I dismounted in the yard.

"You've given her enough," usually signifies "you've given her too much." But I opined not, and we walked round to the house tolerably well convinced that the approaching banking transactions would be on the right side of the book.

Despite a walk with Nellie, and the arrival of a pile of music from town, the afternoon passed rather slowly; perhaps we were too anxious to be cheerful. To make matters worse, dinner was to be postponed till past eight, for the aunt was coming, and Nellie was afraid the visitor would be offended if they did not wait for her.

"You look very bored and tired, sir!" said Nellie pouting prettily; "I believe you'd yawn if it wasn't rude!"

I assured her that I could not, under any circumstances, be guilty of such an enormity.

"It's just a quarter past seven. We'll go and meet the carriage, and then perhaps you'll be able to keep awake until dinnertime!" and so with a look of dignity which would have been very effective if the merry smile in her eyes had been less apparent, the little lady swept out of the room; to return shortly arrayed in furs, and a most coquettish-looking hat, and the smallest and neatest possible pair of boots, which in their efforts to appear strong and sturdy only made their extreme delicacy more decided.

"Come, sleepy boy!" said she, holding out a grey-gloved hand. I rose submissively, and followed her out of the snug drawing-room to the open air.

Bertie was outside, smoking.

"We are going to meet the aunt, dear," explained Nellie. "I'm afraid she'll be cross, because it's so cold."

"She's not quite so inconsequent as that, I should fancy; but it is cold, and isn't the ground hard!" I said.

"It *is* hard!" cried Bertie, stamping vigorously. "By Jove! I hope it's not going to freeze!" and afflicted by the notion — for a hard frost would have rendered it necessary to postpone the races — he hurried off to the stables, to consult one of the men who was weather-wise.

Some stone steps led from the terrace in front of the house to the lawn; at either end of the top-step was a large globe of stone, and on to one of these thoughtless little Nellie climbed. I stretched out my hand, fearing that the weather had made it slippery, but before I could reach her she slipped and fell.

"You rash little person!" I said, expecting that she would spring up lightly.

"Oh! my foot!" she moaned; and gave a little shriek of pain as she put it to the ground.

I took her in my arms, and summoning her maid, carried her to the drawing-room.

"Take off her boot," I said to the girl, but Nellie could not bear to have her foot touched, and feebly moaned that her arm hurt her.

"Oh! pray send for a doctor, sir!" implored the maid, while Nellie only breathed heavily, with half-closed eyes; and horribly frightened, I rushed off, hardly waiting to say a word to the poor little sufferer.

"Whatever is the matter?" Bertie cried, as I burst into the harness-room.

"Where's the doctor?" I replied, hastily. "Nellie's hurt herself — sprained her ankle, and hurt her arm — broken it, perhaps!"

"How? When?" he asked.

"There's no time to explain. She slipped down. Where's the doctor?"

"Our doctor is ill, and has no substitute. There's no one nearer than Lawson, at Oakley, and that's twelve miles, very nearly."

"Then I must ride at once," I reply.

"Saddle my horse as quickly as possible," said Bertie to the groom.

"He's lame, sir, can't move!" the man replied, and I remembered that it was so.

"Put a saddle on one of the carriage horses — anything so long as there's no delay."

"They're out, sir! Gone to the station. There's nothing in the stable — only the mare; and to gallop her to Oakley over the ground as it is to-night, will pretty well do for her chance to-morrow — to say nothing of the twelve miles back again. The carriage will be home in less than an hour, sir," the man remonstrated.

"It may be, you don't know, the trains are

so horridly unpunctual. Saddle the mare, Jarvis, as quickly as you can — every minute may be of the utmost value!" As Bertie spoke the *faintest* look of regret showed itself on his face for a second; for of course he knew that such a journey would very materially affect, if it did not entirely destroy, the mare's chance.

Jarvis, who I think had been speculating, very reluctantly took down the saddle and bridle from their pegs, but I snatched them from his arms, and assisted by Bertie, was leading her out of the stable in a very few seconds.

"Hurry on! Never mind the mare — good thing she's in condition," said Bertie, who only thought now of his sister. "I'll go and see the girl."

"I can cut across the fields, can't I, by the cross roads?" I asked, settling in the saddle.

"No! no! Keep to the highway; it's safer at night. Go on!" I heard him call as I went at a gallop down the cruelly hard road.

The ground rang under the mare's feet, and in spite of all my anxiety for Nellie I could not help feeling one pang of regret for Little Lady, whose free, bounding action, augured well for what her chances would have been on the morrow — chances which I felt were rapidly dying out; for if

259

this journey didn't lame her nothing would. Stones had just been put down as a matter of course; but there was no time for picking the way, and taking tight hold of her head we sped on.

About a mile from the Lodge I came to the crossroads. Before me was a long vista of stone — regular rocks, so imperfectly were they broken: to the right was the smoother and softer pathway over the fields — perfect going in comparison to the road. Just over this fence, a hedge, and with hardly another jump I should come again into the highway, saving quite two miles by the cut. Bertie had said "Don't," but probably he had spoken thoughtlessly, and it was evidently the best thing to do, for the time I saved might be of the greatest value to poor little suffering Nellie! I pulled up, and drew the mare back to the opposite hedge. She knew her work thoroughly. Three bounds took her across the road: she rose — the next moment I was on my back, shot some distance into the field, and she was struggling up from the ground. There had been a post and rail whose existence I had not suspected, placed some six feet from the hedge on the landing side. She sprang up, no legs were broken; and I, a good deal shaken and confused, rose to my feet, wondering what to do next. I had not had time to collect my thoughts when I heard the rattle of a trap on the road; it speedily approached, and the moonlight revealed the jolly features of old Tom Heathfield, a friendly farmer.

"Accident, sir?" he asked, pulling up. "What! Mr Vaughan!" as he caught sight of my face. "What's the —— why! that ain't the mare, sure-*lie*?"

All the neighbourhood was in a ferment of excitement about the races, and the sight of Little Lady in such a place at such a time struck horror to the honest old farmer.

"Yes, it is — I'm sorry to say. Miss Peyton has met with an accident. I was going for the doctor, and unfortunately there was nothing else in the stable."

"You was going to Oakley, I s'pose, sir? It'll be ruination to the mare. Miss Peyton hurt herself! I'll bowl over, sir; it won't take long; this little horse o' mine can trot a good 'un; and I can bring the doctor with me. The fences, there, is mended with wire. You'd cut the mare to pieces."

"I can't say how obliged to you I am ——"

"Glad of the opportunity of obliging Miss Peyton, sir; she's a real lady!" He was just starting when he checked himself. "There's a little public house about a hundred yards further on; if you don't mind waiting there I'll send Smithers to look at the mare. I pass his house. All right, sir."

His rough little cob started off at a pace for which I had not given it credit; and I slowly followed, leading the mare towards the glimmering light which Heathfield had pointed out. My charge stepped out well, and I didn't think that there was anything wrong, though glad, of course, to have a professional opinion.

A man was hanging about the entrance to the public house, and with his assistance the mare was bestowed in a kind of shed, half cow-house, half stable; and as the inside of the establishment did not look by any means inviting, I lit a cigar and lounged about outside, awaiting the advent of Smithers.

He didn't arrive; and in the course of wandering to and fro I found myself against a window. Restlessly I was just moving away when a voice inside the room repeated the name of *Blankney*. I started, and turning round, looked in.

It was a small apartment, with a sanded floor, and two persons were seated on chairs before the fire conversing earnestly. One of them was a middle-aged man, clad in a brown great-coat with a profusion of fur-collar and cuffs which it would scarcely be libel to term "mangy." He was the owner of an unwholesome-looking face, decorated as to the chin with a straggling crop of bristles which he would have probably termed an imperial.

"Wust year I ever 'ad!" he exclaimed (and a broken pane in the window enabled me to hear distinctly). "The Two Thousand 'orse didn't run; got in deep over the Derby; Hascot was hawful; and though I had a moral for the Leger, it went down."

His own morals, judging from his appearance and conversation, appeared to have followed the example of that for the Leger.

"I can't follow your plans about this race down here, though," said his companion, a younger man, who seemed to hold the first speaker in great awe despite his confessions of failure. "Don't you say that this young Blankney's horse can't get the distance?"

"I do. He never was much good, I 'ear; never won nothing, though he's run in two or three hurdle-races; and since Phil Kelly's been preparing of 'im for this race he's near about broke down. His legs swell up like bolsters after his gallops; and he can't get three miles at all, I don't believe, without he's pulled up and let lean agin something on the journey to rest hisself."

"And yet you're backing him?"

"And yet I'm backing of him."

"This young Peyton's mare can't be worse?" said the younger man, interrogatively.

"That mare, it's my belief, would be fancied for the Grand National if she was entered, and some of the swells saw 'er. She's a real good 'un!" replied the man with the collar.

"I see. You've got at her jockey. You're an artful one, you are."

As the jockey to whom they alluded, I was naturally much interested.

"No, I ain't done that, neither. He's a gentleman, and it's no use talkin' to such as 'im. They ain't got the sense to take up a good thing when they see it — though, for the matter o' that, most of the perfessionals is as bad as the gentlemen. All's fair in love and war," says I; "and this 'ere's war."

"Does Blankney know how bad his horse is?"

"No, bless yer! That ain't Phil Kelly's game." (Kelly was, I knew, the man who had charge of my opponent's horse.)

"Well, then, just explain, will you; for *I* can't see."

From the recesses of his garment the elder man pulled out a short stick about fifteen inches in length, at the end of which was a loop of string; and from another pocket he produced a small paper parcel.

"D'yer know what that is? That's a 'twitch.' D'yer know what that is? That's medicine. I love this 'ere young feller's mare so much I'm a-goin' to give it some nicey med'cine myself; and this is the right stuff. I've been up to the 'ouse today, and can find my way into the stable to-night when it's all quiet. Just slip this loop over 'er lip, and she'll open 'er mouth. Down goes the pill, and as it goes down the money goes into my pocket. Them officer fellers and their friends have been backing Blankney's 'orse; but Phil Kelly will take care that they hear at the last moment that he's no good. Then they'll rush to lay odds on the mare — and the mare won't win."

They laughed, and nudged each other in the side, and I felt a mighty temptation to rush into the room and nudge their heads with my fist. Little Lady's delicate lips, which Nellie had so often petted, to be desecrated by the touch of such villains as these!

While struggling to restrain myself a hand was laid on my shoulders, and, turning round, I saw Smithers. We proceeded to the stable; and I hastily recounted to him what

265

had happened, and what I had heard, as he examined the mare by the aid of a bull's-eye lantern. He passed his hand very carefully over her, whilst I looked on with anxious eyes.

"She's knocked a bit of skin off here, you see." He pointed to a place a little below her knee, and drawing a small box from his pocket, anointed the leg. "But she's all right. All right, ain't you, old lady?" he said, patting her; and his cheerful tone convinced me that he was satisfied. "We'll lead her home. I'll go with you, sir; and it's easy to take means to prevent any games to-night."

When we reached home the doctor was there, and pronounced that, with the exception of a sprained ankle, Nellie had sustained no injury.

Rejoicing exceedingly, we proceeded to the stable; Heathfield, who heard my story, and who was delighted at the prospect of some fun, asking permission to accompany us.

"Collars" had doubtless surveyed the premises carefully, for he arrived about eleven o'clock, and clambered quietly and skilfully into the hayloft above the stable, after convincing himself that all was quiet inside. He opened the trap-door, and down came a foot and leg, feeling about to find a resting-place on the partition which divided Little Lady's loose box from the other stalls. Bertie and I took hold of the leg, and assisted him down, to his intense astonishment; while Heathfield and a groom gave chase to, and ultimately captured his friend, the watcher on the threshold.

"If I'm well enough to do *anything* I'm well enough to lie on the sofa; and there's really *no* difference between a sofa and an easy-chair — if my foot is resting — and I'm sure the carriage is *easier* than *any* chair; and it can't matter about my foot being an inch or two higher or lower — and as for shaking, that's all nonsense. It's very unkind *indeed* of you not to want to take me; and if you won't, directly you've gone I'll get up, and walk about, *and stamp*!"

Thus Nellie, in answer to advice that she should remain at home. How it ended may easily be guessed; and though we tried to be dignified, as we drove along, to punish her for her wilfulness, her pathetic little expressions of sorrow that she should "fall down, and hurt herself, and be such a trouble to everybody," and child-like assurances that she would "not do it again," soon made us smile, and forget our half-pretended displeasure. So with the aunt to take care of her, in case Bertie and I were insufficient, we reached the course.

The first three races were run and then the card said: —

3•15 Match, £120 a side, over the Steeple-chase Course, about three miles and a half.

1. Mr Blankney, 14th Dragoons, ch. h. Jibboom, 5 years, 11 st. 7 lb., rose, black and gold cap.
2. Mr Peyton, b. m. Little Lady, 6 years, 11 st., sky-blue, white cap.

Blankney was sitting on the regimental drag, arrayed in immaculate boots and breeches, and, after the necessary weighing ceremony had been gone through he mounted the great Jibboom, which Phil Kelly had been leading about: the latter gentleman had a rather anxious look on his face; but Blankney evidently thought he was on a good one, and nodded confidently to his friends on the drag as he lurched down the course.

Little Lady was brought up to me, Smithers being in close attendance.

"I *shall* be so glad, if you win," Nellie found opportunity to whisper.

"What will you give me?" I greedily inquire.

"*Anything* you ask me," is the reply; and my heart beats high as, having thrown off my light wrapper and mounted, Little Lady bounds down the course, and glides easily over the hurdle in front of the stand.

Bertie and Smithers were waiting at the starting-post; and, having shaken hands with Blankney, to whom Bertie introduced me, I went apart to exchange the last few sentences with my friends.

Bertie is a trifle pale, but confident; and Smithers seems to have a large supply of the latter quality. In however high esteem we hold our own opinions, we are glad of professional advice when it comes to the push; and I seek instructions.

"No, sir, don't you wait on him. Go away as hard as you can directly the flag drops. I don't like the look of that chestnut's legs — or, rather, I *do* like the look of them for our sakes. Go away as hard as ever you can; but take it easy at the fences; and, excuse me, sir, but just let the mare have her head when she jumps, and she'll be all right. People talk about 'lifting horses at their fences:' I only knew one man who could do it, and he made mistakes."

I nod; smiling as cheerfully as anxiety will

permit me. The flag falls, and Little Lady skims over the ground, the heavy chestnut thundering away behind.

Over the first fence — a hedge — and then across a ploughed field; rather hard going, but not nearly so bad as I expected it would have been: the mare moving beautifully. Just as I reach the second fence a boy rushes across the course, baulking us; and before I can set her going again Jibboom has come up level, and is over into the grass beyond a second before us; but I shoot past and again take up the running. Before us are some posts and rails — rather nasty ones; the mare tops them, and the chestnut hits them hard with all four legs. Over more grass; and in front, flanked on either side by a crowd of white faces, is the water-jump. I catch hold of her head and steady her; and then, she rises, flies through the air, and lands lightly on the other side. A few seconds after I hear a heavy splash; but when, after jumping the hurdle into the course, I glance over my shoulder, the chestnut is still pounding away behind. As I skim along past the stand the first time round and the line of carriages opposite, I catch sight of a waving white handkerchief: it is Nellie; and my confused glimpse imperfectly reveals Bertie and Smithers standing on the box of the carriage.

I had seen visions of a finish, in which a certain person clad in a light-blue jacket had shot ahead just in the nick of time, and landed the race by consummate jockeyship after a neck-and-neck struggle for the last quarter of a mile. This did not happen, however, for, as I afterwards learned, the chestnut refused a fence before he had gone very far, and, having at last been got over, came to grief at the posts and rails the second time round. Little Lady cantered in alone; Blankney strolling up some time afterwards.

There is no need to make record of Bertie's delight at the success. We dined next day at the mess of the 14th, Blankney and his brethren were excessively friendly, and seemed pleased and satisfied; as most assuredly were we. Blankney opines that he went rather too fast at the timber; but a conviction seemed to be gaining ground towards the close of the evening that he had not gone fast enough at any period of the race.

And for Nellie? She kept her promise, and granted my request; and very soon after the ankle was well we required the services of other horses — grey ones!

LITTLE SURE SHOT

Here's a little change of pace that draws on many of the ideas we've been talking about, plus this one: unlike some other sports and physical activities riding has always been enjoyed by both sexes equally. For a while, it was a woman who showed the public and her peers "how it's done."

Little Sure Shot was born Phoebe Ann Mosey on August 13, 1860, in a cabin near what is now Willowdell, Ohio. At the age of eight, she began hunting to feed her widowed mother and siblings. She met and married marksman Frank Butler in 1882 and, together, they joined Buffalo Bill's Wild West attraction three years later.

She was Annie Oakley, one of the most famous and celebrated entertainers of the nineteenth century. Her shooting was so precise she earned the nickname "Little Sure Shot," and I mention her in a book about horses because, boy howdy, in addition to being able to shoot a cigarette from her husband's mouth, that five-foot-tall Ohioan could really ride.

Some of her exploits have taken on the proportions of myth, specifically her ability to hit targets while riding sidesaddle and jumping a fence; or to stand on the back of the horse and take out a series of targets.

No, I have not done these. I haven't even tried. I haven't even been tempted to try. But that doesn't change the fact that both are possible.

Riding sidesaddle, she would have had one foot in a stirrup, with the other leg hooked around sort of a cloth, so she was maintaining her balance that way. In fact, that would have been the only way, because they thought it was unladylike for her to ride with spread legs. Mind you, sidesaddle is a very, very difficult balance but not impossible. And if you trained, got yourself used to it — and a lot of ladies did, since that was the customary way to ride — then you could also shoot a rifle.

Yes — even if you were jumping at the same time.

Every horse takes power strides, three strides before the jump, and in the rhythm of that jump, when you come to the top of the jump, there's a moment of peace and quiet. At the very apex there's a momentary hesitation in the forces of nature: the jump forces that propelled you forward and up are equal, and the forces that are bringing you over and down are not yet assumed. At that instant, everything is briefly but absolutely still. You, the horse, the target . . .

Everything.

Just before reaching the top of that arc, she would bring the rifle up, and she would have no problem hitting a target in that fleeting moment of calm and balance. Timed with almost supernatural perfection. For a young lady whose survival had depended on hitting small, moving targets for dinner, those skills were in muscle memory. It was a matter of constant practice to sharpen them.

That practice-makes-perfect idea is also true when you're standing on horseback, though the mechanics are somewhat different. It's no longer just a matter of timing. Now you're having to use your legs, your knees, your ankles, your thighs, your hips — essentially employing every part of you that flexes in order to maintain your shoulders at a steady rate and position. Imagine how important the soles of your feet become, since those are the antennae that inform the rest of your body how to countermove. It's not like standing on shifting beach sands or a train. It's more like standing on the roof of a car . . . and trying to shoot a playing card that's being flipped in the air, or a lighted candlewick.

Make no mistake, this was an amazing woman, deservedly one of the most admired Americans of her age.

Her employer was also pretty impressive, a man whose real-life exploits have been overshadowed by a pulp-fiction legend: William F. Cody.

THE LIFE OF HON. WILLIAM F. CODY, KNOWN AS BUFFALO BILL, THE FAMOUS HUNTER, SCOUT AND GUIDE, AN AUTOBIOGRAPHY

BY WILLIAM F. CODY (1879)

William F. "Buffalo Bill" Cody was a showman. In print, in a stage show, and in his Wild West show — this wonderful horseman and hero presented only the legend the public craved, not the less operatic hero he truly was. Thus, we have no idea how many of his "autobiographical" escapades were even remotely true.

Like this one:

"Yes, he's a California horse; he was captured there wild," replied father.

The exhibition of horsemanship given by Billings on this occasion was really wonderful, and was the most skillful and daring feat of the kind that I ever witnessed. The remainder of the evening was spent around the camp, and Horace, who remained there, entertained us with several interesting chapters of his experiences.

Next morning he walked over to his own

camp, but soon returned, mounted on a beautiful horse, with a handsome saddle, bridle and lariat. I thought he was a magnificent looking man. I envied his appearance, and my ambition just then was to become as skillful a horseman as he was. He had rigged himself out in his best style in order to make a good impression on his uncle at Weston, whither father and I accompanied him on horseback.

He was cordially received by Uncle Elijah, who paid him every possible attention, and gave me a handsome saddle and bridle for my pony, and in the evening when we rode out to the farm to see my mother and sisters, I started ahead to show them my present, as well as to tell them who was coming. They were delighted to see the long-lost Horace, and invited him to remain with us. When we returned to camp next day, Horace settled up with the proprietor of the horses, having concluded to make his home with us for that summer at least.

Father employed him in cutting house logs and building houses, but this work not being adapted to his tastes, he soon gave it up, and obtained government employment in catching United States horses. During the previous spring the government herd had stampeded from Fort Leavenworth, and between two and three hundred of the horses were running at large over the Kansas prairies, and had become quite wild. A reward of ten dollars was offered for every one of the horses that was captured and delivered to the quartermaster at Fort Leavenworth. This kind of work of course just suited the roaming disposition of Billings, especially as it was similar to that in which he had been engaged in California. The horses had to be caught with a lasso, with which he was very expert. He borrowed Little Gray, who was fleet enough for the wildest of the runaways, and then he at once began his horse hunting.

Everything that he did, I wanted to do. He was a sort of hero in my eyes, and I wished to follow in his footsteps. At my request and with father's consent, he took me with him, and many a wild and perilous chase he led me over the prairie. I made rapid advances in the art of horsemanship, for I could have had no better teacher than Horace Billings. He also taught me how to throw the lasso, which, though it was a difficult thing to learn, I finally became quite skillful in.

Whenever Horace caught one of the horses which acted obstinately, and would not be led, he immediately threw him to the ground, put a saddle and bridle on him, and gave me Little Gray to take care of. He would then mount the captive horse and ride him into Fort Leavenworth. I spent two months with Horace in this way, until at last no more of the horses were to be found. By this time I had become a remarkably good rider for a youth, and had brought both of my ponies under easy control.

Horace returned to assist father in hauling logs, which were being used in building a dwelling for the family who had moved over from Missouri. One day a team did not work to suit him, and he gave the horses a cruel beating. This greatly displeased father, who took him to task for it. Horace's anger flew up in a moment; throwing down the lines he hurried to the house, and began packing up his traps. That same day he hired out to a Mormon train, and bidding us all good-bye started for Salt Lake, driving six yokes of oxen.

As a storm was coming up it was quite dark, and the scouts feared that they would lose the way; besides it was a dangerous ride, as a large party of Indians were known to be camped on Walnut Creek, on the direct road to Fort Hays. It was evident that Curtis was trying to induce me to volunteer. I made some evasive answer to Curtis, for I did not care to volunteer after my long day's ride. But Curtis did not let the matter drop. Said he:

"I wish, Bill, that you were not so tired by your chase of to-day, for you know the country better than the rest of the boys, and I am certain that you could go through."

"As far as the ride to Fort Hays is concerned, that alone would matter but little to me," I said, "but it is a risky piece of work just now, as the country is full of hostile Indians; still if no other scout is willing to volunteer, I will chance it. I'll go, provided I am furnished with a good horse. I am tired of being chased on a government mule by Indians." At this Captain Nolan, who had been listening to our conversation, said:

"Bill, you may have the best horse in my company. You can take your choice if you will carry these dispatches. Although it is against regulations to dismount an enlisted man, I have no hesitancy in such a case of urgent necessity as this is, in telling you that you may have any horse you may wish."

"Captain, your first sergeant has a splendid horse, and that's the one I want. If he'll let me ride that horse, I'll be ready to start in one hour, storm or no storm," said I.

"Good enough, Bill; you shall have the

horse; but are you sure you can find your way on such a dark night as this?"

"I have hunted on nearly every acre of ground between here and Fort Hays, and I can almost keep my route by the bones of the dead buffaloes," I confidently replied.

"Never fear, Captain, about Cody not finding the way; he is as good in the dark as he is in the daylight," said Curtis.

An orderly was sent for the horse, and the animal was soon brought up, although the sergeant "kicked" a little against letting him go. After eating a lunch and filling a canteen with brandy, I went to headquarters and put my own saddle and bridle on the horse I was to ride. I then got the dispatches, and by ten o'clock was on the road to Fort Hays, which was sixty-five miles distant across the country. The scouts had all bidden me a hearty good-bye, and wished me success, not knowing when, if ever, they would again gaze upon "my warlike form," as the poet would say.

It was dark as pitch, but this I rather liked, as there was little probability of any of the red-skins seeing me unless I stumbled upon them accidentally. My greatest danger was that my horse might run into a hole and fall down, and in this way get away from me. To avoid any such accident, I tied one end of my rawhide lariat to the bridle and the other end to my belt. I didn't propose to be left on foot, alone out on the prairie.

It was, indeed, a wise precaution that I had taken, for within the next three miles the horse, sure enough, stepped into a prairie-dog's hole, and down he went, throwing me clear over his head. Springing to his feet, before I could catch hold of the bridle, he galloped away into the darkness; but when he reached the full length of the lariat, he found that he was picketed to Bison William. I brought him up standing, and after finding my gun, which had dropped to the ground, I went up to him and in a moment was in the saddle again, and went on my way rejoicing keeping straight on my course until I came to the ravines leading into Walnut Creek, twenty-five miles from Fort Larned, where the country became rougher, requiring me to travel slower and more carefully, as I feared the horse might fall over the bank, it being difficult to see anything five feet ahead. As a good horse is not very apt to jump over a bank, if left to guide himself, I let mine pick his own way. I was now proceeding as quietly as possible, for I was in the vicinity of a band of Indians who had recently camped in that locality. I thought that I had passed somewhat above the spot, having made a little circuit to the west with that intention; but as bad luck would have it this time, when I came up near the creek I suddenly rode in among a herd of horses. The animals became frightened and ran off in every direction.

I knew at once that I was among Indian horses, and had walked into the wrong pew; so without waiting to apologize, I backed out as quickly as possible. At this moment a dog, not fifty yards away, set up a howl, and then I heard some Indians engaged in conversation; — they were guarding the horses, and had been sleeping. Hearing my horse's retreating footsteps toward the hills, and thus becoming aware that there had been an enemy in their camp, they mounted their steeds and started for me.

I urged my horse to his full speed, taking the chances of his falling into holes, and guided him up the creek bottom. The Indians followed me as fast as they could by the noise I made, but I soon distanced them; and then crossed the creek.

When I had traveled several miles in a straight course, as I supposed, I took out my compass and by the light of a match saw that I was bearing two points to the east of north. At once changing my course to the direct route, I pushed rapidly on through the darkness towards Smoky Hill River. At about three o'clock in the morning I began traveling more cautiously, as I was afraid of running into another band of Indians. Occasionally I scared up a herd of buffaloes or antelopes, or coyotes, or deer, which would frighten my horse for a moment, but with the exception of these slight alarms I got along all right.

After crossing Smoky Hill River, I felt comparatively safe as this was the last stream I had to cross. Riding on to the northward I struck the old Santa Fe trail, ten miles from Fort Hays, just at break of day.

My horse did not seem much fatigued, and being anxious to make good time and get as near the post as possible before it was fairly daylight as there might be bands of Indians camped along Big Creek, I urged him forward as fast as he could go. As I had not "lost" any Indians, I was not now anxious to make their acquaintance, and shortly after *reveille* rode into the post. I proceeded directly to General Sheridan's headquarters, and, was met at the door, by Colonel Moore, *aid-de-camp* on General Sheridan's staff who asked me on what business I had come.

"I have dispatches for General Sheridan, and my instructions from Captain Parker, commanding Fort Larned, are that they shall be delivered to the General as soon as possible," said I.

Colonel Moore invited me into one of the offices, and said he would hand the dispatches to the General as soon as he got up.

"I prefer to give these dispatches to General Sheridan myself, and at once," was my reply.

The General, who was sleeping in the same building, hearing our voices, called out, "Send the man in with the dispatches." I was ushered into the General's presence, and as we had met before he recognized me and said:

"Hello, Cody, is that you?"

"Yes, sir; I have some dispatches here for you, from Captain Parker," said I, as I handed the package over to him.

He hurriedly read them, and said they were important; and then he asked me all about General Hazen and where he had gone, and about the breaking out of the Kiowas and Comanches. I gave him all the information that I possessed, and related the events and adventures of the previous day and night.

"Bill," said he, "you must have had a

pretty lively ride. You certainly had a close call when you ran into the Indians on Walnut Creek. That was a good joke that you played on old Satanta. I suppose you're pretty tired after your long journey?"

"I am rather weary, General, that's a fact, as I have been in the saddle since yesterday morning;" was my reply, "but my horse is more tired than I am, and needs attention full as much if not more," I added. Thereupon the General called an orderly and gave instructions to have my animal well taken care of, and then he said, "Cody, come in and have some breakfast with me."

"No, thank you, General," said I, "Hays City is only a mile from here, and I prefer riding over there, as I know about every one in the town, and want to see some of my friends."

"Very well; do as you please, and come to the post afterwards as I want to see you," said he.

Bidding him good-morning, and telling him that I would return in a few hours, I rode over to Hays City, and at the Perry House I met many of my old friends who were of course all glad to see me. I took some refreshments and a two hours nap, and afterward returned to Fort Hays, as I was requested.

THE BLUE GRASS SEMINARY GIRLS' VACATION ADVENTURES; OR, SHIRLEY WILLING TO THE RESCUE

BY CAROLYN JUDSON BURNETT (1916)

Ms. Burnett wrote a number of novels about "the Blue Grass Seminary Girls." Perhaps she was inspired by the exploits of Annie Oakley; if so, she was not alone. Horses (and adolescent love) were everywhere in these stories for and about young ladies. For example, this excerpt from *The Outdoor Girls in the Saddle* (1922), by Laura Lee Hope:

And Andy Rawlinson, flashing his pleasant smile, flung himself from his mount, while the beautiful horse stood there, quivering, head hung in shame ——

"Game hoss, that," said Andy, as he vaulted the low railing and approached the girls. "Fought like a thoroughbred."

"And you were wonderful," cried Betty, with her warm impulsiveness. "I never saw finer riding. We were all afraid you were going to be killed."

Here is a self-contained chapter from one of those novels about a horse to the rescue.

Chapter I. — The Broken Dam.

"The dam! The dam! The dam has broken!"

Shirley Willing, with flaming eyes and tightly-clenched hands, jumped quickly forward, and with her right hand seized the bridle of a horse that was bearing a strange boy along the road, which ran near the river.

The horse reared back on its haunches, frightened at the sudden halting.

"The dam!" cried the young girl again. "Quick! The people must be warned!"

The face of the rider turned white.

"What do you mean?" he shouted, fear stamped on every feature.

Shirley's excitement fell from her like a cloak. She became quiet.

"The Darret dam has been washed away," she answered, "and unless the people in the valley are warned immediately they will perish. There is one chance to save them. You are mounted. You can outrun the oncoming wall of water and save them. Away with you, quick! There is not a second to spare!"

"But," protested the boy, "the water may overtake me and I shall drown. We can climb to higher ground here and be safe."

He tried to turn his horse's head to the east. But Shirley clung to the rein.

"And leave those people to drown, without warning?" she cried. "You coward! You are afraid!"

"I ——" the boy began, but Shirley cut his protest short.

Releasing the bridle of the horse, she sprang quickly to the side of the animal, seized the rider by the leg with both her strong, young hands and pulled quickly and vigorously. Unprepared for such action, the boy came tumbling to the ground in a sprawling heap.

Quick as a flash Shirley leaped to the saddle and turned the horse's head toward the valley. As she dug her heels into the animal's ribs, sending him forward with a jump, she called over her shoulder to the boy, who sat still dazed at the sudden danger:

"Get to safety the best way you can, you coward!"

Under the firm touch of the girl's hand on the rein the horse sped on down the valley.

It was a mad race with death and Shirley knew it. But she realized that human lives were at stake and she did not hesitate.

To the left of the road down which she sped lay high ground and safety, while coming down the valley, perhaps a mile in the rear, poured a dense wall of water, coming as swift as the wind.

For days the Mississippi and its tributaries had been rising rapidly and steadily. Along the lowlands in that part of the state of Illinois, just south of Cairo, where Shirley Willing had been visiting friends, fears that the Darret dam, three miles up one of these tributary streams, would give way, had been entertained.

Some families, therefore, had moved their perishable belongings to higher ground, where they would be beyond the sweep of the waters should the dam break.

Then suddenly, without warning, the dam had gone.

The home where Shirley had been visiting was a farmhouse, and the cry of danger had been received by telephone. Those in the house had been asked to repeat the warning to families further down the valley. But the fierce wind that was raging had, at almost that very moment, blown down all wires.

Shirley, in spite of the fact that she, with the others, could easily have reached the safety afforded by higher ground a short distance away, had thought only of those whose lives would be snuffed out if they were not warned.

She had decided that she would warn

them herself. She ran from the house to the stable, where one single horse had been left.

But the seriousness of the situation seemed to have been carried to the animal, and when Shirley had attempted to slip a bridle over his head he struck out violently with his fore feet. As the girl sprang back, he dashed from the stable.

Shirley ran after him and followed him into the road. There she encountered a rider; and the conversation with which this story begins took place.

As the girl sped down the road, she could hear from far behind the roar of the waters as they came tumbling after her.

A farmhouse came into sight. A man, a woman and several children came out, attracted by the galloping hoof beats. Without checking the speed of her mount a single instant, Shirley guided the horse close to them.

"The dam! The dam!" she shouted, as she flashed by.

No other words were necessary. Without stopping to gather up any of their effects, they all turned their faces and rushed for higher ground.

A second, a third, and a fourth farmhouse came into view, and as she flashed by, the girl hurled her warning at each.

Half a mile below lay the little town of Stanley. It was for this that Shirley was headed, in her race with the rushing water.

The roar behind her became louder, and Shirley, leaning over her horse's neck, urged him to further efforts with soft and coaxing words.

The noble animal, seeming to realize that he was upon a message of life or death, responded, and it seemed that he must have winged feet, so lightly and swiftly did he fly over the ground.

But the roaring wall of water came closer.

Shirley uttered a cry of relief. Before her she made out the first house in the little town. The sounds of the clattering hoofs on the hard macadamized road drew the residents from their homes. Several had gathered in a little knot as Shirley approached. Evidently they had not heard the sound of the roaring waters.

"The dam has gone!" cried the girl, as she came up to them, and rode by without checking the speed of her horse. "Fly for your lives!"

Instantly all became bustle and confusion. The word was passed like a flash and almost as one man the town poured from its homes and dashed for safety.

Clear through the town the young girl

rode, calling out her warning. Then, and not until then, did she check her horse and turn his head toward the safety that lay in the east.

A man ran up to her.

"The Hendersons!" he cried. "They left here not five minutes ago in their buggy. The water will catch them on the road!"

Without a word, Shirley turned her horse and would have dashed forward had not the man caught the bridle.

"It's death to you!" he cried.

"It's death to them if I don't make it!" cried Shirley.

She dug her heels into the animal's flanks and the horse shook off the detaining hand with a quick twitch of his head. Evidently he, as well as the girl, realized his responsibility.

Once more, under the guiding hand, he dashed forward as if it were wings that carried him so lightly and swiftly over the ground. And as he flew on, Shirley patted him softly on the neck and spoke low words of encouragement.

The noble animal's ears stood straight and there was fire in his eyes. He seemed to say: "We will save them if it is possible."

Rounding a sudden turn in the road, Shirley made out a buggy going leisurely along. At the same moment the roar of the water came more plainly to her ears.

She raised her voice in a shout that rose above the sound of roaring water behind — rose above the sounds of clattering hoofs and above the voices of the occupants of the buggy themselves.

The buggy stopped, the man's face peered out. As he saw Shirley dashing along the road after him, a sudden understanding of what was wrong came to him. Raising an arm, he waved it as a signal that the girl's warning had been understood, and started his horse on a run.

Shirley breathed a great sigh of relief and dashed on after the buggy, which was now going at terrific speed, rocking crazily and threatening every moment to turn over in the road.

Coming suddenly to an open field at the left side of the road, the man sent the buggy dashing across it, and made, as fast as his horse could go, for a point where the ground rose sheer for perhaps a hundred feet.

Shirley sped after the buggy.

Coming to this abrupt rise, they were forced to search for a means of clambering up it. The woman in the buggy, at the man's command, sprang from the seat and dashed hurriedly up the steep hill. The man in the meantime stopped to unhitch his horse, that the animal might have a chance for its life.

Turning in her saddle, Shirley cried out in sudden fear.

Behind, so close that it seemed to be right upon her and bearing down with tremendous speed, came a solid wall of water, many feet high.

With a cry to her horse, the girl turned his head squarely to the hill. With his nostrils extended and his eyes dilated with fear, the animal sprang at it. With his light burden he gained a foothold and dashed up as fast as his weary limbs could carry him. Once he came to a place that seemed too much for him; but the noble steed made a last desperate effort and succeeded in getting his forefeet on top of the level ground above.

With a single movement, Shirley flung herself from the saddle to the safety of the high ground, and in another moment seized the bridle of the horse, just as he would have slipped back into the raging flood that now swept by below.

Exerting her utmost strength — and it was by no means slight — she succeeded in helping the animal to scramble to the summit.

The occupants of the buggy had also succeeded in climbing to safety, but the second horse had been carried away by the sweeping waters. Henderson had been unable to loosen the animal, as he was forced to hurry to the support of Mrs. Henderson, who, almost in safety, had fainted and would have fallen back, had her husband's arm not caught her.

From this refuge, the three watched the waters as they swirled by with tremendous force. Kicking animals, sheds, barns and small houses, together with ruins and débris, swept past them, and more than once the young girl cried out in despair, as she realized the damage that had been done by the water.

The three had climbed to the very top of the hill, as the water surrounded them on all sides. Gradually it rose, climbing closer and closer to them. Shirley became alarmed and turned to Henderson, who stood near her, still supporting his wife.

"Will it come this high, do you think, Mr. Henderson?"

Henderson shook his head.

"There is no telling," he replied quietly. "All we can do is to hope for the best."

All became silent, but their eyes were

riveted upon the water as it closed in on them.

Now there was but perhaps twenty yards of dry ground, then fifteen, and still the water rose. The rise continued until all stood in water, and then it rose no higher.

"Thank God!" said Henderson, calmly, looking at his wife. "We are saved!"

"Thank God, indeed," said Shirley softly, and she turned and stroked the horse, who thrust his cold muzzle into her hand. "But for you," she added, patting him gently, "hundreds would have been drowned!"

BORN IN THE SADDLE

Born in the saddle.

It's just an expression. It describes someone, like Annie Oakley, who is such a good and natural rider that — well, they had to have been born on horseback. Indeed, in some cases, it may be true in a literal sense.

In Asia, Cossacks and Mongolian horsemen were (and remain) among the finest riders who ever lived. They are always jumping off the horse, running alongside it, getting back on, spinning on their butts on top of the horse. Through it all, there is remarkably little leg contact. What are they using to control the horse . . . or is that just a ridiculously well-trained horse?

The answer is: both.

Among certain people — and you can include Native American riders among them — the horse's sides are so sensitized that just the slightest shift in weight is all you need to cue the horse that it has to do something. The Native Americans didn't have a saddle, and they sat on the horse using — in totality — the bounce, and the grip of their legs on the horse. Native American children would grow up riding a horse, becoming one with the horse. They were a little mean on the withers of the horse, clinging there, with their hands in the mane. They wrapped their legs around the horse in whatever fashion they could, depending on the reach and strength of their thighs, shins, feet. Riding bareback is a skill involving a level of balance that you only partially use in a saddle. When riding with a saddle, if the horse suddenly stops, using the saddle and your balance and your instincts, your feet shoot forward in the stirrups, and you resist the forces of nature, gravity, by the soles of your feet, and you push back with your legs and thighs. You resist the forward g-force of a sliding horse. Without a saddle, you don't have that option.

I frankly do not know how you prevent yourself from going over the head of a horse when that horse, at full gallop, decides to turn left or right, or suddenly stops and braces all four feet in front of a hole and says, "I'm not going over that hole." Many great horsemen have come off a horse when it resists a jump, even if they're using a saddle. Every jumper Grand Prix horse I've ever seen, at a full gallop, with a great horseman on his back, who resists a jump invariably causes the horseman to go over the horse's head and hit the ground, or hit the jump.

How the heck does the horseman without a saddle not do that? Maybe they did fall. Maybe more Native Americans and Mongols and Cossacks were injured than we know. That's certainly not something one would memorialize in art.

However, there is also the possibility — and it happens to me every day that I am on one of my horses — that they are reading your mind. Or something very close to that. Remember my mentioning before about the horse that knew his trainer was coming, however much she changed her pattern? In some strange fashion, it might be some imperceptible muscle twitch that you're totally unaware of — but the moment you think of doing something, the horse is prepared to do it.

A little historical sidebar here to validate that point. It's about a horse named Clever Hans. He was an Orlov Trotter who lived at the turn of the twentieth century, and this horse was touted as being able to add up figures. His owner, Wilhelm von Osten, would bring him to circuses where people would pay to ask something like, "What's seven and seven, what's two and nine, what's fourteen plus twenty," and the horse would paw to the sum and then stop. The crowds and the owner actually believed the horse could add and subtract. They tried blindfolding Clever Hans, they tried blindfolding and muting the owner. And the horse would add up those figures.

The trainer swore that he was doing nothing, and people kept their eyes on him. He was doing nothing. It was only years and years later that they discovered that the horse, who just happened to paw continuously, would do so until given a cue not to. What was happening on an extremely subtle level was that when the horse arrived at the figure, the trainer or an engaged observer either took in or let out a breath in anticipation or relief. It was inadvertent and it was there, since his livelihood depended on it! The horse took that as a command to stop. That was how he got to the correct figure.

My friend the martial artist, whom I mentioned earlier, has been training for sixty years and he calls these barely perceptible disturbances "micro-movements." He says that a seasoned martial artist, a master, is not someone who goes into a situation

301

with grand, showy moves. He approaches with incredible stillness. He watches for a tic, a blink, a breath, the movement of a toe or finger or a shift in stance. Then he will strike, decisively.

Any experienced horseman will tell you the same thing about riding. You force yourself, move yourself, think yourself into an absolutely relaxed position. No cue from your legs or butt at all. And many, many horses seem to sense what you want. So if you are thinking about changing leads, that horse has got your thought.

These people who are born in the saddle probably understand that before they understand the actual mechanics of horse control. They also understand the psychology of horses — and by extension, all animals they might encounter, from steer to mules to sheep.

All animals — and let's open this up to orcas, lions, lowland gorillas, elephants, mountain goats — they're highly, highly intelligent, highly intuitive. There are scientists who say that we anthropomorphize all these animals, all these qualities we think of as "human," and that none of that exists. But an equal number of ethologists will tell you that animals not only have rudimentary reasoning capabilities, they also have morality.

You can see this yourself. When animals play, they make a significant signal. For example, birds. You can always tell the difference between those that are courting and, say, pigeons that are puffing up to dominate a ledge or a crust of bread in the street. Dogs bow as if to announce, "Okay, it's playtime. So when I bite you I won't be biting you for real." And every so often they reassure each other, "Hey, this is for play." When one or the other exceeds that play, they won't press the advantage and cause more harm. They will make a sign that says, "This is play, but I've bit you too hard, you yelped, and now I have to say 'I'm sorry' or we've got a problem. Because the play just turned into something more fearful." You'll notice that they are always, ineffably gentle around babies. When dogs do try to assert themselves —

Here's something that happened to me very recently. I had just come in from riding and this little terrier was there. He belonged to a guest; I hadn't seen him before. I walked into the tack room and he started barking and then he attacked me! He actually jumped at my leg and started nipping, the way terriers do. I yelled at him and he backed into the corner growling and yelping, and I growled and yelped right back at him! I dominated him. And finally he gave up and he cowered down a little bit, and then he came up to me and I gave him my hand, and I petted him, and I absolutely communicated with that terrier: "You don't do that to me." I wasn't cruel, I wasn't mean, I just did what dogs would do and he understood that this was not his turf.

So, based on a number of indicators, we can divine that in all animals there is a sense of fair play. Yes, of course, some of that — as with the terrier — is rooted in survival. But as soon as we established a dialogue, there was actual détente! And the higher up you go — on the chain of what we think are the higher animals — the more that takes place. Humans who put their vanity aside, who access their animal core — and we all do have one, genetically speaking — can read this very, very clearly.

With that groundwork laid, I want to talk about two exceptional show-business figures who were born in the saddle.

One was a stuntman by the name of Yakima Canutt. Born in 1895, he was a champion rodeo rider before he went into movies as a stuntman. He is credited (by himself, anyway) with having given his pal

John Wayne his distinctive walk.

Maybe he did, maybe he didn't. He was certainly among those who taught the Duke to ride well. Yak himself definitely walked "that way," with an almost equine sway. Rodeo riding will do that — give you a constant shift in your step, a realignment, a change in your balance.

It takes a long time to move that fluidly, and developing the skills to stay on a bucking horse requires a *lot* of falls. You have to learn not to fear it and to be relaxed enough to stay on the horse. So if you're looking at a guy sitting on a bucking horse, he's fallen off countless times. It's a metaphoric cliché, of course, getting right back on the horse after you've been thrown. But it's true, and it takes something special to get back on that independent-minded titan. I've been bucked off more times than I can count and, frankly, I don't know how these rough riding folks can stay on. That horse is tossing so hard and fast that you leave gravity. That's right: you get flung upward, first, by the transfer of energy and when you come down the saddle is just coming up. You hit it hard, it hurts, and you're off. If you manage to hang on, your balance is completely gone in the first leap or two. So I don't know how these guys stay on a bucking horse, but they do.

Well, that's not quite true. Yak and others stay on a bucking horse because it's what they were born to do.

Yak loved horses. *Loved* them. He was so good at controlling them with nuance that he was one of the few people who could look credible on horseback firing a rifle or shooting a bow and arrow for the camera. He also invented an entirely new kind of "horse fall" in Westerns, one in which the rider took the horse down in a way that injured neither horse nor rider. When John Ford made *Stagecoach* in 1939, the joke — which wasn't really a joke — was that Yak was the one who took the fall for every galloping cavalryman, stagecoach rider, and Native American in the climactic chase. That same year, Yak doubled for Clark Gable during the burning-of-Atlanta scene in *Gone with the Wind.* Not just because of the fire danger, but in order to coax the horse to move past a conflagration of that size and intensity. Watch that scene: it's amazing how Yak gets that horse to move.

This man was born for that work. He was one with his horses, something we'll talk more about later.

The other film personality I want to mention here was a wonderful horseman named

Ben Johnson. Ben was a tall, toned guy who worked as a ranch hand, rodeo rider, and wrangler for films before becoming an actor. You may remember him roping a gorilla in *Mighty Joe Young* in 1949. When he was too old to do the kind of hard riding he did in films, he became a wonderful character actor who won the Best Supporting Actor Oscar for his work in the 1971 film *The Last Picture Show.*

You watch an actor riding a horse on-screen — follow the horse with your eye, you will see those actors who can ride and those who can't. I talked a little about this earlier, but watch how unskilled riders jerk the reins. What happens is the horse's mouth gets really sensitive, especially when they might have to do the scene two, three, four, five times. The horse anticipates what's going to happen, and you can see that on-screen. But then you see someone like Ben Johnson, who was a cowboy, or other skilled rider/actors like Tyrone Power, Randolph Scott, Errol Flynn, Gary Cooper, Tab Hunter, Tim Holt, Charlton Heston — their horses' heads never move no matter how many takes were required, because the rider was in control. They are constantly talking to the horse through the reins.

They are the epitome of great riders,

people who make the art look relaxed and easy.

My hat is off in tribute to those riders, to Annie Oakley and others, who inspire us still.

How the Old Horse Won the Bet

BY OLIVER WENDELL HOLMES (1830)

The bond between horse and rider is an elusive quality, and this poem gets it right.

Author, poet, physician — Oliver Wendell Holmes (1809–1894) was one of the great persons of his age. I came across this poem many years ago in his collection The One Horse Shay (1891), and there was never any doubt that I would include it in this collection.

It isn't just the wonderful, masterly writing and storytelling: it is the theme itself, which certainly speaks to those of us well beyond our middle age. I would add that it is miraculous, too, in that the title tells you how it ends and yet you will still keep reading!

'T was on the famous trotting-ground,
The betting men were gathered round
From far and near; the "cracks" were there
Whose deeds the sporting prints declare:
The swift g. m., Old Hiram's nag,
The fleet s. h., Dan Pfeiffer's brag,
With these a third — and who is he

That stands beside his fast b. g.?
Budd Doble, whose catarrhal name
So fills the nasal trump of fame.

There too stood many a noted steed
Of Messenger and Morgan breed;
Green horses also, not a few;
Unknown as yet what they could do;
And all the hacks that know so well
The scourgings of the Sunday swell.

Blue are the skies of opening day;
The bordering turf is green with May;
The sunshine's golden gleam is thrown
On sorrel, chestnut, bay, and roan;
The horses paw and prance and neigh,
Fillies and colts like kittens play,
And dance and toss their rippled manes
Shining and soft as silken skeins;
Wagons and gigs are ranged about,
And fashion flaunts her gay turn-out;
Here stands, — each youthful Jehu's
    dream, —
The jointed tandem, ticklish team!

And there in ampler breadth expand
The splendors of the four-in-hand;
On faultless ties and glossy tiles
The lovely bonnets beam their smiles;
(The style's the man, so books avow;

The style's the woman, anyhow;)
From flounces frothed with creamy lace
Peeps out the pug-dog's smutty face,
Or spaniel rolls his liquid eye,
Or stares the wiry pet of Skye; —
O woman, in your hours of ease
So shy with us, so free with these!

"Come on! I'll bet you two to one
I'll make him do it!" "Will you? Done!"

What was it who was bound to do?
I did not hear and can't tell you, —
Pray listen till my story's through.

Scarce noticed, back behind the rest,
By cart and wagon rudely prest,
The parson's lean and bony bay
Stood harnessed in his one-horse shay —
Lent to his sexton for the day;
(A funeral — so the sexton said;
His mother's uncle's wife was dead.)

Like Lazarus bid to Dives' feast,
So looked the poor forlorn old beast;
His coat was rough, his tail was bare,
The gray was sprinkled in his hair;
Sportsmen and jockeys knew him not,
And yet they say he once could trot
Among the fleetest of the town,

311

Till something cracked and broke him
   down, —
The steed's, the statesman's, common lot!
"And are we then so soon forgot?"
Ah me! I doubt if one of you
Has ever heard the name "Old Blue,"
Whose fame through all this region rung
In those old days when I was young!

"Bring forth the horse!" Alas! he showed
Not like the one Mazeppa rode;
Scant-maned, sharp-backed, and
   shaky-kneed,
The wreck of what was once a steed,
Lips thin, eyes hollow, stiff in joints;
Yet not without his knowing points.
The sexton laughing in his sleeve,
As if 't were all a make-believe,
Led forth the horse, and as he laughed

Unhitched the breeching from a shaft,
Unclasped the rusty belt beneath,
Drew forth the snaffle from his teeth,
Slipped off his head-stall, set him free
From strap and rein, — a sight to see!

So worn, so lean in every limb,
It can't be they are saddling him!
It is! his back the pig-skin strides
And flaps his lank, rheumatic sides;

312

With look of mingled scorn and mirth
They buckle round the saddle-girth;
With horsey wink and saucy toss
A youngster throws his leg across,
And so, his rider on his back,
They lead him, limping, to the track,
Far up behind the starting-point,
To limber out each stiffened joint.

As through the jeering crowd he past,
One pitying look old Hiram cast;
"Go it, ye cripple, while ye can!"
Cried out unsentimental Dan;
"A Fast-Day dinner for the crows!"
Budd Doble's scoffing shout arose.

Slowly, as when the walking-beam
First feels the gathering head of steam,
With warning cough and threatening
      wheeze
The stiff old charger crooks his knees;
At first with cautious step sedate,
As if he dragged a coach of state;
He's not a colt; he knows full well
That time is weight and sure to tell;
No horse so sturdy but he fears
The handicap of twenty years.

As through the throng on either hand
The old horse nears the judges' stand,

Beneath his jockey's feather-weight
He warms a little to his gait,
And now and then a step is tried
That hints of something like a stride.

"Go!" — Through his ear the summons
    stung
As if a battle-trump had rung;
The slumbering instincts long unstirred
Start at the old familiar word;
It thrills like flame through every limb —
What mean his twenty years to him?
The savage blow his rider dealt
Fell on his hollow flanks unfelt;
The spur that pricked his staring hide
Unheeded tore his bleeding side;
Alike to him are spur and rein, —
He steps a five-year-old again!

Before the quarter pole was past,
Old Hiram said, "He's going fast."
Long ere the quarter was a half,
The chuckling crowd had ceased to laugh;
Tighter his frightened jockey clung
As in a mighty stride he swung,
The gravel flying in his track,
His neck stretched out, his ears laid back,
His tail extended all the while
Behind him like a rat-tail file!

Off went a shoe, — away it spun,
Shot like a bullet from a gun;
The quaking jockey shapes a prayer
From scraps of oaths he used to swear;
He drops his whip, he drops his rein,
He clutches fiercely for a mane;

He'll lose his hold — he sways and reels —
He'll slide beneath those trampling heels!
The knees of many a horseman quake,
The flowers on many a bonnet shake,
And shouts arise from left and right,
"Stick on! Stick on!" "Hould tight! Hould
    tight!"
"Cling round his neck and don't let go —"
"That pace can't hold, — there! steady!
    whoa!"
But like the sable steed that bore
The spectral lover of Lenore,
His nostrils snorting foam and fire,
No stretch his bony limbs can tire;
And now the stand he rushes by,
And "Stop him! — stop him!" is the cry.

Stand back! he's only just begun, —
He's having out three heats in one!

"Don't rush in front! he'll smash your brains;
But follow up and grab the reins!"
Old Hiram spoke. Dan Pfeiffer heard,

And sprang impatient at the word;
Budd Doble started on his bay,
Old Hiram followed on his gray,
And off they spring, and round they go,
The fast ones doing "all they know."

Look! twice they follow at his heels,
As round the circling course he wheels,
And whirls with him that clinging boy
Like Hector round the walls of Troy;
Still on, and on, the third time round!
They're tailing off! they're losing ground!

Budd Doble's nag begins to fail!
Dan Pfeiffer's sorrel whisks his tail!
And see! in spite of whip and shout,
Old Hiram's mare is giving out!
Now for the finish! at the turn,
The old horse — all the rest astern, —
Comes swinging in, with easy trot;
By Jove! he's distanced all the lot!

That trot no mortal could explain;
Some said, "Old Dutchman come again!"
Some took his time, — at least they tried,
But what it was could none decide;
One said he couldn't understand
What happened to his second hand
One said 2.10; *that* couldn't be —
More like two twenty two or three;

Old Hiram settled it at last;
"The time was two — too dee-vel-ish fast!"

The parson's horse had won the bet;
It cost him something of a sweat;
Back in the one-hoss shay he went;
The parson wondered what it meant,
And murmured, with a mild surprise
And pleasant twinkle of the eyes,
"That funeral must have been a trick,
Or corpses drive at double-quick;
I shouldn't wonder, I declare,
If brother — Jehu — made the prayer!"

And this is all I have to say
About that tough old trotting bay.
Huddup! Huddup! G' lang! — Good-day!

Moral for which this tale is told:
A horse *can* trot, for all he's old.

FOUR HORSES AND A SAILOR

The Human Drift
BY JACK LONDON (1917)

Though he died at the tragically young age of forty, Jack London was a social activist and a war correspondent, and he owned a sprawling ranch in Sonoma County, California, of which he wrote, "Next to my wife, the ranch is the dearest thing in the world to me." London died at that ranch of, among other things, a recurring illness he had picked up in the Klondike.

What a life. And what an author, who wrote such classics as *The Call of the Wild, White Fang,* and the unforgettable short tale of survival "To Build a Fire."

He understood animals and he understood that elusive essence of "place," the interaction I spoke of — human, animal, terrain. This book would not have been complete without him.

I have left the spelling as I found it . . . as he wished it!

"Huh! Drive four horses! I wouldn't sit behind you — not for a thousand dollars — over them mountain roads."

So said Henry, and he ought to have known, for he drives four horses himself.

Said another Glen Ellen friend: "What? London? He drive four horses? Can't drive one!"

And the best of it is that he was right. Even after managing to get a few hundred miles with my four horses, I don't know how to drive one. Just the other day, swinging down a steep mountain road and rounding an abrupt turn, I came full tilt on a horse and buggy being driven by a woman up the hill. We could not pass on the narrow road, where was only a foot to spare, and my horses did not know how to back, especially up hill. About two hundred yards down the hill was a spot where we could pass. The driver of the buggy said she didn't dare back down because she was not sure of the brake. And as I didn't know how to tackle one horse, I didn't try it. So we unhitched her horse and backed down by hand. Which was very well, till it came to hitching the horse to the buggy again. She didn't know how. I didn't either, and I had depended on her knowledge. It took us about half an hour, with frequent debates and consultations, though it is an absolute certainty that never in its life was that horse hitched in that particular way.

No; I can't harness up one horse. But I can four, which compels me to back up again to get to my beginning. Having selected Sonoma Valley for our abiding place, Charmian and I decided it was about time we knew what we had in our own county and the neighbouring ones. How to do it, was the first question. Among our many weaknesses is the one of being old-fashioned. We don't mix with gasoline very well. And, as true sailors should, we naturally gravitate toward horses. Being one of those lucky individuals who carries his office under his hat, I should have to take a typewriter and a load of books along. This put saddle-horses out of the running. Charmian suggested driving a span. She had faith in me; besides, she could drive a span herself. But when I thought of the many mountains to cross, and of crossing them for three months with a poor tired span, I vetoed the proposition and said we'd have to come back to gasoline after all. This she vetoed just as emphatically, and a deadlock obtained until I received inspiration.

"Why not drive four horses?" I said.

"But you don't know how to drive four horses," was her objection.

I threw my chest out and my shoulders

320

back. "What man has done, I can do," I proclaimed grandly. "And please don't forget that when we sailed on the *Snark* I knew nothing of navigation, and that I taught myself as I sailed."

"Very well," she said. (And there's faith for you!) "They shall be four saddle horses, and we'll strap our saddles on behind the rig."

It was my turn to object. "Our saddle horses are not broken to harness."

"Then break them."

And what I knew about horses, much less about breaking them, was just about as much as any sailor knows. Having been kicked, bucked off, fallen over backward upon, and thrown out and run over, on very numerous occasions, I had a mighty vigorous respect for horses; but a wife's faith must be lived up to, and I went at it.

King was a pole pony from St. Louis, and Prince a many-gaited love-horse from Pasadena. The hardest thing was to get them to dig in and pull. They rollicked along on the levels and galloped down the hills, but when they struck an upgrade and felt the weight of the breaking-cart, they stopped and turned around and looked at me. But I passed them, and my troubles began. Milda was fourteen years old, an unadulterated broncho, and in temperament was a combination of mule and jack-rabbit blended equally. If you pressed your hand on her flank and told her to get over, she lay down on you. If you got her by the head and told her to back, she walked forward over you. And if you got behind her and shoved and told her to "Giddap!" she sat down on you. Also, she wouldn't walk. For endless weary miles I strove with her, but never could I get her to walk a step. Finally, she was a manger-glutton. No matter how near or far from the stable, when six o'clock came around she bolted for home and never missed the directest cross-road. Many times I rejected her.

The fourth and most rejected horse of all was the Outlaw. From the age of three to seven she had defied all horsebreakers and broken a number of them. Then a long, lanky cowboy, with a fifty-pound saddle and a Mexican bit had got her proud goat. I was the next owner. She was my favourite riding horse. Charmian said I'd have to put her in as a wheeler where I would have more control over her. Now Charmian had a favourite riding mare called Maid. I suggested Maid as a substitute. Charmian pointed out that my mare was a branded range horse, while hers was a near-thoroughbred, and that the legs of her mare would be ruined forever if she were driven for three months. I acknowledged her mare's thoroughbredness, and at the same time defied her to find any thoroughbred with as small and delicately-viciously pointed ears as my Outlaw. She indicated Maid's exquisitely thin shinbone. I measured the Outlaw's. It was equally thin, although, I insinuated, possibly more durable. This stabbed Charmian's pride. Of course her near-thoroughbred Maid, carrying the blood of "old" Lexington, Morella, and a streak of the super-enduring Morgan, could run, walk, and work my unregistered Outlaw into the ground; and that was the very precise reason why such a paragon of a saddle animal should not be degraded by harness.

So it was that Charmian remained obdurate, until, one day, I got her behind the Outlaw for a forty-mile drive. For every inch of those forty miles the Outlaw kicked and jumped, in between the kicks and jumps finding time and space in which to seize its team-mate by the back of the neck and attempt to drag it to the ground. Another trick the Outlaw developed during that drive was suddenly to turn at right angles in the traces and endeavour to butt its team-mate over the grade. Reluctantly and nobly did Charmian give in and consent to the use of Maid. The Outlaw's shoes were pulled off, and she was turned out on range.

Finally, the four horses were hooked to the rig — a light Studebaker trap. With two hours and a half of practice, in which the excitement was not abated by several jack-poles and numerous kicking matches, I announced myself as ready for the start. Came the morning, and Prince, who was to have been a wheeler with Maid, showed up with a badly kicked shoulder. He did not exactly show up; we had to find him, for he was unable to walk. His leg swelled and continually swelled during the several days we waited for him. Remained only the Outlaw. In from pasture she came, shoes were nailed on, and she was harnessed into the wheel. Friends and relatives strove to press accident policies on me, but Charmian climbed up alongside, and Nakata got into the rear seat with the typewriter — Nakata, who sailed cabin-boy on the *Snark* for two years and who had shown himself afraid of nothing, not even of me and my amateur jamborees in experimenting with new modes of locomotion. And we did very nicely, thank you, especially after the first hour or so, during which time the Outlaw had kicked about fifty various times, chiefly to the damage of her own legs and the paintwork, and after she had bitten a couple of hundred times, to the damage of Maid's neck and Charmian's temper. It was hard enough to have her favourite mare in the harness without also enduring the spectacle of its being eaten alive.

Our leaders were joys. King being a pole pony and Milda a rabbit, they rounded curves beautifully and darted ahead like coyotes out of the way of the wheelers. Milda's besetting weakness was a frantic desire not to have the lead-bar strike her hocks. When this happened, one of three things occurred: either she sat down on the lead-bar, kicked it up in the air until she got her back under it, or exploded in a straight-ahead, harness-disrupting jump. Not until she carried the lead-bar clean away and danced a break-down on it and the traces, did she behave decently. Nakata and I made the repairs with good old-fashioned bale-rope, which is stronger than wrought-iron any time, and we went on our way.

In the meantime I was learning — I shall not say to tool a four-in-hand — but just simply to drive four horses. Now it is all right enough to begin with four work-horses pulling a load of several tons. But to begin with four light horses, all running, and a light rig that seems to outrun them — well, when things happen they happen quickly. My weakness was total ignorance. In particular, my fingers lacked training, and I made the mistake of depending on my eyes to handle the reins. This brought me up against a disastrous optical illusion. The bight of the off head-line, being longer and heavier than that of the off wheel-line, hung lower. In a moment requiring quick action, I invariably mistook the two lines. Pulling on what I thought was the wheel-line, in order to straighten the team, I would see the leaders swing abruptly around into a jack-pole. Now for sensations of sheer impotence, nothing can compare with a jack-pole, when the horrified driver beholds his leaders prancing gaily up the road and his wheelers jogging steadily down the road, all at the same time and all harnessed together and to the same rig.

I no longer jack-pole, and I don't mind admitting how I got out of the habit. It was my eyes that enslaved my fingers into ill practices. So I shut my eyes and let the fingers go it alone. To-day my fingers are independent of my eyes and work automatically. I do not see what my fingers do. They just do it. All I see is the satisfactory result.

Still we managed to get over the ground that first day — down sunny Sonoma Valley to the old town of Sonoma, founded by General Vallejo as the remotest outpost on the northern frontier for the purpose of holding back the Gentiles, as the wild Indians of those days were called. Here history was made. Here the last Spanish mission was reared; here the Bear flag was raised; and here Kit Carson, and Fremont, and all our early adventurers came and rested in the days before the days of gold.

We swung on over the low, rolling hills, through miles of dairy farms and chicken ranches where every blessed hen is white, and down the slopes to Petaluma Valley. Here, in 1776, Captain Quiros came up Petaluma Creek from San Pablo Bay in quest of an outlet to Bodega Bay on the coast. And here, later, the Russians, with Alaskan hunters, carried skin boats across from Fort Ross to poach for sea-otters on the Spanish preserve of San Francisco Bay. Here, too, still later, General Vallejo built a fort, which still stands — one of the finest examples of Spanish adobe that remain to us. And here, at the old fort, to bring the chronicle up to date, our horses proceeded to make peculiarly personal history with astonishing success and dispatch. King, our peerless, pole-pony leader, went lame. So hopelessly lame did he go that no expert, then and afterward, could determine whether the lameness was in his frogs, hoofs, legs, shoulders, or head. Maid picked up a nail and began to limp. Milda, figuring the day already sufficiently spent and maniacal with manger-gluttony, began to rabbit-jump. All that held her was the bale-rope. And the Outlaw, game to the last, exceeded all previous exhibitions of skin-removing, paint-marring, and horse-eating.

At Petaluma we rested over while King was returned to the ranch and Prince sent to us. Now Prince had proved himself an excellent wheeler, yet he had to go into the lead and let the Outlaw retain his old place. There is an axiom that a good wheeler is a poor leader. I object to the last adjective. A good wheeler makes an infinitely worse kind of a leader than that. I know . . . now. I ought to know. Since that day I have driven Prince a few hundred miles in the lead. He is neither any better nor any worse than the first mile he ran in the lead; and his worst is even extremely worse than what you are thinking. Not that he is vicious. He is merely a good-natured rogue who shakes hands for sugar, steps on your toes out of sheer excessive friendliness, and just goes on loving you in your harshest moments.

But he won't get out of the way. Also, whenever he is reproved for being in the wrong, he accuses Milda of it and bites the back of her neck. So bad has this become that whenever I yell "Prince!" in a loud voice, Milda immediately rabbit-jumps to the side, straight ahead, or sits down on the lead-bar. All of which is quite disconcerting. Picture it yourself. You are swinging round a sharp, down-grade, mountain curve, at a fast trot. The rock wall is the outside of the curve. The inside of the curve is a precipice. The continuance of the curve is a narrow, unrailed bridge. You hit the curve, throwing the leaders in against the wall and making the pole horse do the work. All is lovely. The leaders are hugging the wall like nestling doves. But the moment comes in the evolution when the leaders must shoot out ahead. They really must shoot, or else they'll hit the wall and miss the bridge. Also, behind them are the wheelers, and the rig, and you have just eased the brake in order to put sufficient snap into the manoeuvre. If ever team-work is required, now is the time. Milda tries to shoot. She does her best, but Prince, bubbling over with roguishness, lags behind. He knows the trick. Milda is half a length ahead of him. He times it to the fraction of a second. Maid, in the wheel, over-running him, naturally bites him. This disturbs the Outlaw, who has been behaving beautifully, and she immediately reaches across for Maid. Simultaneously, with a fine display of firm conviction that it's all Milda's fault, Prince sinks his teeth into the back of Milda's defenceless neck. The whole thing has occurred in less than a second. Under the surprise and pain of the bite, Milda either jumps ahead to the imminent peril of harness and lead-bar, or smashes into the wall, stops short with the lead-bar over her back, and emits a couple of hysterical kicks. The Outlaw invariably selects this moment to remove paint. And after things are untangled and you have had time to appreciate the close shave, you go up to Prince and reprove him with your choicest vocabulary. And Prince, gazelle-eyed and tender, offers to shake hands with you for sugar. I leave it to any one: a boat would never act that way.

But to return to the horses. There is some improvement. Milda has actually learned to walk. Maid has proved her thoroughbredness by never tiring on the longest days, and, while being the strongest and highest spirited of all, by never causing any trouble save for an occasional kick at the Outlaw.

And the Outlaw rarely gallops, no longer butts, only periodically kicks, comes in to the pole and does her work without attempting to vivisect Maid's medulla oblongata, and — marvel of marvels — is really and truly getting lazy. But Prince remains the same incorrigible, loving and lovable rogue he has always been.

And the country we've been over! The drives through Napa and Lake Counties! One, from Sonoma Valley, via Santa Rosa, we could not refrain from taking several ways, and on all the ways we found the roads excellent for machines as well as horses. One route, and a more delightful one for an automobile cannot be found, is out from Santa Rosa, past old Altruria and Mark West Springs, then to the right and across to Calistoga in Napa Valley. By keeping to the left, the drive holds on up the Russian River Valley, through the miles of the noted Asti Vineyards to Cloverdale, and then by way of Pieta, Witter, and Highland Springs to Lakeport. Still another way we took, was down Sonoma Valley, skirting San Pablo Bay, and up the lovely Napa Valley. From Napa were side excursions through Pope and Berryessa Valleys, on to Ætna Springs, and still on, into Lake County, crossing the famous Langtry Ranch.

At Usal, many hilly and picturesque miles north of Fort Bragg, we turned again into the interior of Mendocino, crossing the ranges and coming out in Humboldt County on the south fork of Eel River at Garberville. Throughout the trip, from Marin County north, we had been warned of "bad roads ahead." Yet we never found those bad roads. We seemed always to be just ahead of them or behind them. The farther we came the better the roads seemed, though this was probably due to the fact that we were learning more and more what four horses and a light rig could do on a road. And thus do I save my face with all the counties. I refuse to make invidious road comparisons. I can add that while, save in rare instances on steep pitches, I have trotted my horses down all the grades, I have never had one horse fall down nor have I had to send the rig to a blacksmith shop for repairs.

Also, I am learning to throw leather. If any tyro thinks it is easy to take a short-handled, long-lashed whip, and throw the end of that lash just where he wants it, let him put on automobile goggles and try it. On reconsideration, I would suggest the substitution of a wire fencing-mask for the goggles. For days I looked at that whip. It fascinated me, and the fascination was composed mostly of fear. At my first attempt, Charmian and Nakata became afflicted with the same sort of fascination, and for a long time afterward, whenever they saw me reach for the whip, they closed their eyes and shielded their heads with their arms.

Here's the problem. Instead of pulling honestly, Prince is lagging back and manoeuvring for a bite at Milda's neck. I have four reins in my hands. I must put these four reins into my left hand, properly gather the whip handle and the bight of the lash in my right hand, and throw that lash past Maid without striking her and into Prince. If the lash strikes Maid, her thoroughbredness will go up in the air, and I'll have a case of horse hysteria on my hands for the next half hour. But follow. The whole problem is not yet stated. Suppose that I miss Maid and reach the intended target. The instant the lash cracks, the four horses jump, Prince most of all, and his jump, with spread wicked teeth, is for the back of Milda's neck. She jumps to escape — which is her second jump, for the first one came when the lash exploded. The Outlaw reaches for Maid's neck, and Maid, who has already jumped and tried to bolt, tries to bolt harder. And all this infinitesimal fraction of time I am trying to hold the four animals with my left hand, while my whip-lash, writhing through the air, is coming back to me. Three simultaneous things I must do: keep hold of the four reins with my left hand; slam on the brake with my foot; and on the rebound catch that flying lash in the hollow of my right arm and get the bight of it safely into my right hand. Then I must get two of the four lines back into my right hand and keep the horses from running away or going over the grade. Try it some time. You will find life anything but wearisome. Why, the first time I hit the mark and made the lash go off like a revolver shot, I was so astounded and delighted that I was paralysed. I forgot to do any of the multitudinous other things, tangled the whip lash in Maid's harness, and was forced to call upon Charmian for assistance. And now, confession. I carry a few pebbles handy. They're great for reaching Prince in a tight place. But just the same I'm learning that whip every day, and before I get home I hope to discard the pebbles. And as long as I rely on pebbles, I cannot truthfully speak of myself as "tooling a four-in-hand."

We still consider our trip is just begun. As soon as this is mailed from Eureka, it's heigh ho! for the horses and pull on. We shall continue up the coast, turn in for Hoopa Reservation and the gold mines, and shoot down the Trinity and Klamath rivers in Indian canoes to Requa. After that, we shall go on through Del Norte County and into Oregon. The trip so far has justified us in taking the attitude that we won't go home until the winter rains drive us in. And, finally, I am going to try the experiment of putting the Outlaw in the lead and relegating Prince to his old position in the near wheel. I won't need any pebbles then.

THE UNCERTAINTY FACTOR

I didn't know Christopher Reeve well.

We met at industry functions, at science-fiction conventions — there was always a fuss about "Captain Kirk Meets Superman" — and of course through our love of horses. I certainly knew him enough to know that he was a good, intelligent, articulate man who was as much in love with his horses as I am with mine. In fact, I am told that he had a clause in his movie contracts that the producers would bring one or more of his horses to the movie sets, no matter where they were, no matter what location it was, so he was able to ride between shots. That's how much he loved this sport, this . . . art.

Chris hadn't sat a horse for sport until he was thirty-three, when he learned to ride to play the dashing Count Vronsky in the film *Anna Karenina.* I've heard that he was immediately struck with a dilemma: he was smitten with horses . . . and allergic to them. He was forced to take antihistamines to ride and — we'll get into this more later — within a few years the allergies went away. Horses do help us to heal.

Anyway, he began training in earnest. Chris studied very hard and he was very, very good. He started eventing and especially loved three-day eventing, which is a very challenging, and somewhat dangerous, sport. It requires great physicality, great stamina in the horse and rider as you make your way up hills, through water, and of course jumping. In every other jumping sport, the rails give way if the horse knocks them. Points are deducted and that's usually the worst of it. But in three-day eventing, those are permanent jumps. Not quite as high as the Grand Prix, but they're usually trees. I'm not exaggerating. I was just at the Kentucky State Park in Lexington last week, running beside these jumps, and they are big gnarly tree trunks. Not only isn't there any give, they're gigantic. They're six feet long, and wide, and four to five feet high, and the horse has to jump over them. And if he scrapes one of them, he scrapes it. But if he hits it, he'll brake himself and the rider will be tossed. If you hit it, if you smash into that trunk — that's tough to walk away from.

An observation, here — the tragic wisdom of hindsight. Chris was a big man, six foot four, and he muscled up to play Superman. The ideal jockey is about five-one, five-two, 110 pounds, very light and exceedingly strong. Men like the fabled Willie Shoemaker are among the best athletes in the world.

Chris had added a lot of muscle on his upper body, which is not what you want when you're into jumping the way he was. And even though he was no longer pumping iron, riding as much as he did is a great way to build stomach muscles, biceps, to expand your chest. So he stayed fit . . . and top-heavy.

In 1994, Chris bought a twelve-year-old Thoroughbred named Eastern Express and he decided to compete in the Commonwealth Dressage and Combined Training Association finals in Culpeper, Virginia. That's a three-day event. While he was jumping, a freak accident happened. The horse refused to go over a jump. It just stopped. Chris was thrown forward, and his hand went into the bridle, tied up, and he couldn't protect himself. He fell on his head on the opposite side of the fence, jamming his spine, breaking his first and second vertebrae. They didn't know at the time how extensive the damage was — he was paralyzed from the neck down — but he also stopped breathing. Paramedics were able to push air into his lungs and, of course, raced him to the hospital.

That news shocked the world and especially the horse world. It was personally very sobering. Despite all the years I spent with horses, I have to confess that for about a six-month period, every time I got on a horse I thought of Chris Reeve. Every time I put a leg over a horse, I thought, "Is this my time to die or be crippled for life?" Even with the passage of time, he was frequently in my thoughts.

Eventually, one day, I was traveling to New York and instead of flying into JFK I flew to Newark, because Chris was at the Kessler Rehabilitation Center in West Orange, New Jersey. I had called ahead and said, "I'd love to come and visit with you." And he said, "I'd be delighted."

Lord, I didn't know how he would react, how I would react. I didn't know what to expect after all this time, the many months that had gone by when he was incommunicado. He couldn't walk, he had no control over his body below his neck, he couldn't even breathe without a ventilator. I tried not to think about what to say or do, just to be there for him, whatever that meant.

I entered through the glass doors of the hospital, and I saw him in the wheelchair. I immediately felt such an identification, such an empathy for him, I could hardly keep the tears from my eyes. He saw that, I'm sure. He must have been used to that.

But I walked over and he spoke first, saying, "Sit down, Bill." So I sat beside him and I couldn't help but notice the battery that operated the lungs, the mechanism that opened and closed his chest. He could only take very short breaths and he had to marshal those to speak. And he said with his first breath, in about three phrases, "Tell me. How your horses are. And how much you love riding."

Those words, the intonation, the longing he put into them — they will stay with me always.

The rest of the evening was all about horses. I cannot say what was in his heart during my visit, but I know what was in his eyes in spite of everything:

Joy.

A MILITARY STEEPLE-CHASE

CAPTAIN R. BIRD THOMPSON,
IN *Sporting Society; or, Sporting Chat
and Sporting Memories, Vol. 1,*
EDITED BY FOX RUSSELL (1897)

I present this story in honor of Chris: a hearty, living, thundering tale. If this were a film, he'd have starred in it with confidence and stature.

According to the original book publication, Thompson was one of "various sporting celebrities and well-known writers on the turf and the chase." He was apparently British, which is implicit in his other writings about angling, duck hunting, and partridge shooting in and around London. Never once does he reveal anything about his military background, other than what can be gleaned from this memoir.

No matter.

It is a delightful read, evocative, once more, of a different time. And, in a way, the last line is probably as good as any as we make our way through life.

We were quartered in a very sporting part of the country, where the hunting season was always wound up by a couple of days' steeple-chasing. The regiment stationed here had usually given a cup for a military steeple-chase, and when we determined to give one for an open military handicap chase, the excitement was very great as to our chances of winning the cup we had given. As there were some very good horses and riders in the regiment, it appeared a fair one, eight nominations having been taken by us. There were also about the same number taken by regiments in the district. Our Major, who was a first-rate horseman, entered his well-known horse Jerry; I and others nominated one each, but one sub., a very celebrated character amongst us, took two. This man's father had made a very large fortune by nursery gardens, and put his son into the army, where, of course, he was instantly dubbed "The Gardener." He was by no means a bad sort of fellow, but he never could ride. The riding-master almost cried as he said he never could make "The Gardener" even look like riding; not that he was destitute of pluck, but he was utterly unable to stick on the horse. He had a large stud of hunters, but when out he almost invariably tumbled off at each fence.

Amongst those who nominated horses was the celebrated Captain Lane, of the Hussars, who was said to be so good a jockey that the professionals grumbled greatly at having to give him amateurs' allowance. No one was better at imperceptibly boring a competitor out of the course; and at causing false starts and balking at fences he was without a rival. The way he would seem to be hard on his horse with his whip, when only striking his own leg, was quite a master-piece. Report declared that he trained all his own horses to these dodges, and I believe it was quite true, as his were quite quiet and cool under the performances when the rest were almost fretted out of their lives.

When the handicap came out I found, to my great disgust, that such a crusher had been put on my horse that I at once put the pen through his name — not caring to run him on the off-chance of his standing up and the rest coming to grief, or with the probability, anyhow, of a punishing finish. However, the next night after mess, the Major called me up to him in the ante-room, and said: "I hear you have scratched your horse, and quite right, too. I have accepted, and if you [would] like to have the mount, you are quite welcome." Of course, I was greatly delighted, but told him that I had never ridden in [a] steeple-chase before. "But I have," growled the Major, "and am not going to waste over this tin-pot," as he irreverently called the cup, "so I can show you the ropes. Come to my quarters after breakfast tomorrow, and we will try the horse."

The next day I went there, and found the Major mounted, awaiting me, and Jerry — a very fine brown horse, with black points. I soon discovered that he had one decided peculiarity — viz., at his first fence, and sometimes the second, instead of going up and taking it straight, he would whip round suddenly and refuse. On thinking what could be the cause of this trick, I came to the conclusion that his mouth must have been severely punished by the curb when he was first taught jumping; and on telling the Major my idea, he allowed me to ride him as I pleased, so instead of an ordinary double bridle, I put one with a couple of snaffles in his mouth, and very soon found that this had the desired effect. Indeed, after a few days, he took his first fence all right, unless flurried, and before the day seemed quite trustworthy.

When we got back after our first day's ride, the Major told me, rather to my amusement, that I must go into training as well as the horse, — adding, what was quite true, that he had seen more amateur races lost through the rider being beat before the horse than by any other means; so when I had given Jerry his gallops in the morning, I had to start a mile run in the afternoon in flannels or sweaters.

The course was entirely a natural one, about three miles and a half round, and only two ugly places in it, chiefly grass, with one piece of light plough and some seeds. The first two fences were wattles on a bank, with a small ditch, then an ordinary quickset hedge, followed by an old and stiff bullfinch. After this a post and rails, a bank with a double ditch, and merely ordinary fences till we came to a descent of about a quarter of a mile, with a stream about twelve feet wide, and a bank on the taking-off side. Next came some grass meadows, with a very nasty trappy ditch, not more than four feet wide, but with not the slightest bank or anything of the kind on either side, — just the thing for a careless or tired horse to gallop into. The last fence, which was the worst of all, was, I fancy, the boundary of some estate or parish, and consisted of a high bank, with a good ditch on each side — on the top a young, quick-set hedge, and, to prevent horses or cattle injuring it, two wattle fences, one on each side, slanting outwards. After this, there was a slight ascent of about 300 yards; then there was dead level of about a quarter of a mile up to the winning-post.

On the evening before the chase, we had a grand guest night, to which, of course, all the officers of other regiments who had entered horses were invited. We youngsters were anxious to see Captain Lane, of whom we had heard so much.

On his arrival, after the usual salutations, he enquired of the Major whether he was going to ride, and, on receiving a negative, asked who was; and on having the intending jockeys pointed out to him, just favoured us with a kind of contemptuous glance, never taking any further notice of us.

The celebrated Captain was a slight man, about five feet eight inches, with not a particularly pleasant look about his eyes, and looking far more the jock than the soldier. The steeple-chases were fixed for the next day at 2.30 P.M., but, as a matter of fact, all the riders were on the ground long before that for the purpose of examining the ground and the fences.

The Major came to see me duly weighed out, and gave me instructions as to riding — that I was not on any account to race with everyone who came alongside me, nor to make the running at first, unless the pace was very slow and muddling, of which there was little danger, for quite half the jocks, he said, would go off as if they were in for a five furlong spin, and not for a four mile steeple-chase.

I was to lie behind, though handy, until we came to the descent to the stream and then make the pace down and home as hot as I could, — to find out the "dicky fore-legs," he said, knowing that Jerry's were like steel.

We all got down to the post pretty punctually, and, of course, in a race of this description, the starter had no difficulty in dropping his flag at the first attempt.

I gave Jerry his head, and to my joy he took the first fence as straight and quietly as possible, so taking a pull at him, I was at once passed by some half dozen men (the gallant "Gardener" amongst them) going as hard as they could tear. It was lucky for them that the fences were light and old, as most of the horses rushed through them. When they got to the bullfinch, one horse refused, and another attempting to, slipped up and lay in a very awkward looking lump, jock and all close under it. The rest having been a little steadied took it fairly enough. Jerry jumped it as coolly as possible, like the regular old stager that he was, in spite of Captain Lane coming up at the time with a great rush, evidently hoping to make him refuse.

When we landed on the other side a ludicrous spectacle presented itself, the gallant "Gardener" being right on his horse's neck, making frantic attempts to get back into his saddle, which were quite unsuccessful, and the horse coming to the next fence, a post and rail, quietly took it standing, then putting down his head slipped his rider off and galloped on without him.

The field now began to come back to us very quickly, and soon the leading lot were Vincent of ours, a splendid rider, as I thought, and as it turned out, my most dangerous opponent, with a Carabinier in close attendance; then myself, with Captain Lane waiting on me, and watching the pair of us most attentively, so that it seemed almost impossible that I should have any chance of slipping him. However, an opportunity did present itself at length, which I took advantage of — hearing a horse coming up a tremendous "rattle" on my right.

I looked round to see who and what it was. Lane, noticing what I was doing, looked round too. Seeing this I loosed Jerry's head, and giving him at the same time a slight touch with the spur, he shot out completely — slipping the Captain, passing the Carabinier, and getting head and head with Vincent. Down the hill we went as hard as we could, clearing the water side by side. At the grip in the fields beyond I gained slightly by not taking a steadier at Jerry, trusting to his eyesight and cleverness to avoid grief.

As we got to the best fence, the ugly boundary one, I did take a pull, the jump looking as nasty a one as could well be picked out; however, the old horse did it safely, and Vincent and myself landed side by side in the winning field, amidst most tremendous shouting and cheering from our men, who were standing as thick as thick could be on each side of the course.

The excitement was terrific as we came up, apparently tied together, but giving Jerry a couple of sharp cuts with the whip, I found my leg gradually passing Vincent's, until at length I was nearly opposite his horse's head, and thus we passed the winning post, to my great relief. I did not know how much my opponent's horse had left in him, and expected him to come up with a rush at the last, in which case I doubted whether I should be able to get anything more out of Jerry in time, as he was rather a lazy horse, though possessing enormous "bottom."

I had scarcely pulled up and turned round to go to the scales, before I met the Major, who told me I was "not to make a fool of myself and dismount," before the clerk of the scales told me to, and then he pitched into me for riding at the "Grip," as I did, apprising me at the same time that he did not care how I risked my neck, but "I might have hurt the horse," adding, after a pause, and with a grunt, "but you won."

The delight of our men was so great at two of their officers being first and second, that it was all that Vincent and myself could do to avoid being carried about on their shoulders after we had weighed in.

The gallant captain was most awfully disgusted at being beaten by "a couple of boys," and went off immediately — resisting all invitations to stop and dine at mess. I subsequently found out that when I slipped him (at which he was particularly angry) he gave his horse a sharp cut with his whip, which seemed quite to upset it.

On coming down to the water the horse jumped short — dropping his hind legs in, and at the "Grip," nearly got in, only saving itself by bucking over it, and at the big boundary absolutely came down on landing, though his rider managed to keep his seat.

As for myself, I need not say how delighted I was at winning my first steeplechase, though the Major did tell me that a monkey would have ridden as well, and helped the horse as much as I did. *"But I won"* was always my reply.

OUR HORSES, OUR SELVES

I love riding in a sulky behind a trotting horse. That's a light, two-wheel, one-horse, one person carriage. I've won championships, and guiding a horse from behind comes somewhat naturally. My muscles knew it quite well, almost from the start. That doesn't mean I was a chariot driver in some hypothetical previous life. For one thing, in a sulky it's like you're on a bike. You're on two parallel wheels and you're pressing into those stirrups . . . it's like you're on a motorcycle. With a chariot, your stance is more like skiing.

It *could* mean that maybe my connection is with the horse itself, spiritually, not through the reins. Or maybe I was a Cossack, challenging myself and a horse on the Russian steppes.

I don't know. But I *do* know I have a connection with horses that I cannot explain.

I was reading, recently, about LUCA: the

last universal common ancestor. According to scientists, this is an organism that lived about four billion years ago around volcanic vents deep in the ocean. These organisms became the ancestor of all life-forms.

Assuming that this is true, all of us — humans, horses, the whole panoply of life — have that in common. Those of us who open up to people, horses, trees, you name it, make special connections with them. Born in the saddle? Green thumb? Maybe it's a matter of being sensitive to some aspect of your own ancient gene pool.

I have talked a lot about spirituality in this book and I know that these energetic connections exist among the living. What about the dead?

When I am in the field where Great Day is buried, I am alone with my memories. There is a Navajo verse about a dead horse, which goes in part:

In the mist of blessed pollen hidden, all
    hidden he;
How joyous his neigh!

I don't feel that — not because I don't want to, but because I've accepted that my bond, my connection through LUCA, is with the living horse. Perhaps when I'm gone, we'll be united, both neighing joyously.

I don't know.

Our concept of death is skewed by what we feel over the loss of another. It is possible, even likely, that the lingering pain of that loss, the refusal to completely surrender that connection, obscures our "outreach" to the departed soul.

I don't know.

Many actors — most? — experience that same thing in a small way when a play closes. You've bonded with other actors, exchanged energy eight times a week, hung around in a cast house, in the dressing rooms, and then, suddenly, it stops. You walk around for a while, looking for a place to put your key. Then, hopefully, another job comes along and you form a new connection. Sometimes you stay in touch with the other actors, have reunions. The connection survives, at least a little.

Not so with death. At least, as far as I can prove.

The irony is, if many paranormal scholars are right, it takes about twenty days for the spirit to find its way to heaven or wherever it is in accordance with one's form of belief. At a time when we could make a connection, in theory, we're blocked, impeded, too busy grieving.

My belief is that a spirit or soul has got to go someplace, somewhere that human-conceived physical, psychological, and ethical rules don't apply. It's way, way beyond that. I believe that when a beloved companion or parent or child or animal dies, it goes *somewhere* — and when you die, you go to that same place. Perhaps the bond you forged in life is what leads you there. Perhaps we're all following that first LUCA. (Though I wonder if those volcanic vents are somehow, in our DNA, the origins of hell?)

There's a reason I bring all this up.

I'll be talking more about the spirituality of the horse in the final chapter. But writing this book, thinking about the spirit of the horse and its relationship to the spirit of human beings, all got me thinking — or rather, not thinking, just feeling: *if* I could time travel, if we had that portal from *Star Trek* in "The City on the Edge of Forever" through which I could just hop somewhen else, where would that be?

Keep in mind, I am a man of the twenty-first century. By that I mean I love to ride, and my favorite rides are those filled with the romance of the West. You go out to a place like Red Rock Canyon in Nevada, and it looks great, epically great, and it's appropriately dusty and dry and harsh. Time vanishes while you're out there. But then, astride my well-conditioned horse, I ride back to a really neat hotel, and I have somebody take care of the horse, and I get in the swimming pool and then have a great dinner. So maybe this question shouldn't be posed to my eighty-six-year-old self, but to a much younger version.

Oddly enough, if I could send that youthful, *White Comanche*–age William Shatner somewhere, it wouldn't be to the time of Alexander or Genghis Khan, though that would be wonderful to witness, of course. It would be to ancient Minoa, which arose on the island of Crete around 3600 BCE. That predates Alexander by three full millennia.

We spoke before about Centaurs, but there were also legends about the Minotaur, the half man, half bull, and you look at these vases and terra-cotta figurines they left behind and read about their history —

These people jumped over bulls. Their culture was such that they did not stick the bulls as a torero does, but they athletically leapt over them, men and women both. And we're not talking about jumping like hurdles. They came at the bull from the front, grabbed the horns, and were typically flung upward by the bull. The leaper would then disengage and land on or behind the bull. It was the ultimate test of courage.

They had horses, too, of course, but as far as I know they only rode those.

When I think of the reckless daring I had in my youth, I think I might like to have been a horseman and athlete in the Minoan culture.

Perhaps I was. Perhaps I will be, yet again, depending on whether reincarnation exists and whether it works backward as well as forward.

Why not?

Which leads to an interesting question: will geneticists one day create a human-horse hybrid?

As an actor in science-fiction pieces, I know something about cloning, about genetically created superhumans. On *Star Trek,* those traditionally did not work out too well.

How would it be, though, if we were to start cloning horses in the real world?

Right now, I'm riding four great horses. In terms of dollars, they're priceless. And by that I mean, in terms of my ability to ride at my age, these horses are invaluable to me. That aside, by any measure, by ability, by temperament, by size, by beauty, and by talent, these horses are great.

If you could clone these horses, if you could get an exact physical replica of each, that would be extremely valuable. A horse starts training at about two years of age. They get really good around eight. And they stay good until about seventeen, eighteen. That's when most of them start to decline and are retired (though not always; I have ridden horses and seen horses that were great up to the age of twenty, twenty-two).

So to have that same stock, as it were, would be a great starting point. If you could clone them you would be getting another horse made of the raw material that made the original horse so great.

On the other hand, you can't clone temperament or talent. That doesn't work. You can only clone physical characteristics. And there's the potential rub.

Horses need three things. First, they need the conformation. That means the perfection or correctness, as it were, of the legs, the body, the head, the shoulders, individually and in their relationship one to the other. If a horse is crooked-legged, it's liable to go lame. If it wings, which is throwing a leg out to the side, then generally it can't run fast, because of its excessive motion. You'll find very few great Thoroughbreds winging.

So conformation is huge. Then there's another thing, and that's talent. Can that horse run, if it's a Thoroughbred? Will that horse jump? Some horses have a talent for some of that, a natural talent. Other horses will refuse to go over a fence or wall. So if he's got conformation and a talent, that's a great start.

The third thing is heart. Some horses resent training. They may not resent it at the beginning. You get them going and say, "My God, that's going to be a great horse." But as you increase the training, many begin to burn out. And at some point the horse says, "I don't want to do this anymore. I am not going to stop when you ask me to stop. I'm not going to jump. I'm going to refuse to jump. Kick me! Hit me! Smack me! I am not going over that jump!"

So horses, like people, need heart. They need talent. And, like human athletes, they need conformation.

Cloning can only guarantee you the conformation. The other two come from countless other factors, interactions, nuances. Right now, cloning those is beyond the ability of science to achieve.

Tomorrow? Who knows. I've written and starred in enough science fiction to know that predicting anything is difficult. There is, however, at least one reliable yardstick: looking back. As we know, as much as things seem to change . . . they don't, really.

"WHOOPING" A RACE-HORSE UNDER THE WIRE

Taking Chances,
BY CLARENCE LOUIS CULLEN (1900)

Here's another tale by Mr. Cullen, who gave us "A Race Horse That Paid a Church Debt." It captures an era long gone with a sport that is nonetheless unchanged.

"I see they hollered an old skate home and got him under the wire first by three lengths out at the Newport merry-go-round the other day," said an old-time trainer out at the Gravesend paddock. "Don't catch the meaning of hollering a horse home? Well, it's scaring a sulker pretty near out of his hide and hair and making him run by sheer force of whoops let out altogether. This nag, Kriss Kringle, that was hollered home at Newport a few days ago, is a sulker from the foot-hills. He was sold as an N. G. last year for $25, and at the beginning of this season he prances in and wins nine or ten

360

straight races right off the reel at the Western tracks, hopping over the best they've got out there. Then he goes wrong, declines to crawl a yard, and is turned out. They yank him into training again awhile back, put him up against the best a-running on the other side of the Alleghanies, and he makes 'em look like bull-pups one day and the next he can't beat a fat man. He comes near getting his people ruled off for in-and-out kidding, and then, a couple of weeks ago, or maybe a bit less, he goes out and chews up the track record, and gets within a second of the world's record for the mile and three-eighths, I believe it was.

"Then, Tuesday they have him in at a mile and a sixteenth, with a real nippy field, as Western horses go. The right people, knowing full well the old Springbok gelding's propensities, shove their big coin in on him anyway, and take a chance on him being unable to keep up with a steam roller after his swell race awhile before, and the whole crowd fall into line and bet on Kringle until the books give them the cold-storage countenance and say, 'Nix, no more.' Then they get up into the stand and around the finishing rail and they see the aged Kriss, who's a rank favorite, begin like a land crab, when he usually goes out from the jump and spread-eagles his bunch. They begin the hard-luck moan when they see the sour son of Springbok trailing along third in a field of five, and they look into each other's mugs and chew about being on a dead one. Turning into the stretch, the old skate is a poor third, and stopping every minute, a plain case of sulks, like he's put up so many times before. The two in front of him have got it right between them, when Kris comes along into the last sixteenth, still third by a little bit, and then the gang let out in one whoop and holler that could be heard four miles. It's 'Wowee! come on here, ye danged old buck-jumper!' and 'Whoop-la! you Kringle!' from nearly every one of the thousand leather lungs in the stand and up against the rail, and the surly old rogue pins his ears forward and hears the yelp. Then it's all off. The old $25 cast-off jumps out like a scared rabbit at the sixteenth-pole. The nearer he gets to the stand the louder the yelping hits him and the bigger he strides; and he collars the two in front of him as if they were munching carrots in their stalls, and romps under the string three lengths to the good. That's what hollering a horse home means. It's a game that can only be worked on sulkers. The yelling scares the sulker into running, whereas it's liable to make a good-dispositioned horse stop as if sand-bagged.

"I've seen the holler-'em-in gag worked often at both the legitimate and the outlaw tracks, and for big money. One of the biggest hog-slaughterings that was ever made at the game was when an Iroquois nag, a six-year-old gelding named McKeever, turned a rank outsider trick at Alexander Island, Va., in 1895. The boys that knew what was going to happen that time surely did buy it by the basketful for a long time afterward. McKeever was worth about $2 in his latter career, and not a whole lot more at any stage of the game, according to my way of sizing 'em. As a five and six-year-old, he couldn't even make the doped outlaws think they were in a race, but his people kept him plugging away on the chance that some day or other he might pick up some of the spirit of his sire, the royal Iroquois, and pay for his oats and rubbing, anyhow. When he was brought to Alexander Island in the spring of '95, and tried out it was seen that he was just the same old truck-mule. One morning, after he'd been beaten a number of times by several Philadelphia blocks, when at 100 to 1 or so in the books, his owner had him out for a bit of a canter around the ring, with a 140-

363

pound stable boy on him. A lot of stable boys and rail birds were scattered all around the infield, assembled in groups at intervals of 100 feet or so, chewing grass and watching the horses at their morning work. This old McKeever starts around the course as if he's doing a sleep-walking stunt. The boy gives him the goad and the bat, but it's no good. McKeever sticks to his caterpillar gait, and his owner leans against the rail with a watch in his mitt and mumbles unholy things about the skate. There's a laugh among the stable boys and the rail birds as McKeever goes gallumphing around. Then a stable lad that's got a bit of Indian in him leans over the rail just as McKeever's coming down, and lets out a whoop that can be heard across the Potomac. McKeever gives a jump, and away he goes like the wind. It looks so funny to the rail birds along the line that they all take up the yelp, and McKeever jumps out faster at every shout. He gets to going like a real, sure-enough race horse by the time he has made the circuit once, and he keeps right on. The owner gets next to it that it's the shouting that's keeping the old plug on the go, and he waves his arms and passes the word along for the boys to keep it up. McKeever does six furlongs in 1:14 with the assistance of the hollering, and the owner takes him off the track, gives him a look-over and some extra attention, and smiles to himself.

"Then he pushes McKeever into a six-and-half furlong race on the following day. He stations about twenty or twenty-five rail birds, all of 'em stable boys out of a job, in the infield, and hands them out their yelling instructions. McKeever is up against one of the best fields of sprinters at the track, and he goes to the post at 30 to 1 and sticks at that. His owner puts a large number of his pals next to what's going to happen, and not a man of them plays the good thing at the track. They have their coin telegraphed in bundles to the poolrooms all over the country. McKeever gets out in front, and he hasn't made more than a dozen jumps before one of the kids inside the rail throws a whoop that makes the people in the stand put their hands to their ears. McKeever gives a swerve and a side step, and away he goes like the Empire State express. A hundred feet further, when he's four lengths in the lead, and the others, including the even money shot, nowhere, a couple more rail birds shoot out another double-jointed yell, and McKeever jumps out again like an ice-yacht. He gets the holler at every 100 feet of his journey, the rail birds not taking any chances on his stopping, although after the first furlong he is six lengths to the good, and the result is that McKeever simply buck-jumps in, pulled double, with eight lengths of open daylight between him and the even money shot. The owner looks sad, like a man who hasn't put a dollar down, and says real hard things to McKeever when the horse is being led to his stable. When he gets him inside his stall, though, the hugs and loaf sugar that fall McKeever's way are a heap. The old-time poolroom people will tell you yet how they had to turn the box, a good many of 'em, the day that McKeever was hollered home at old Alexander Island.

"And, talking about Alexander Island, there were some funny ones yanked off over there, sure enough, some of them almost as funny as a few that happened over in New York at the legit tracks this passing season. Without hurling out any names, I'll just tell you of how a plunger who has been a good deal talked about this year, on account of his big winnings, got the dump-and-the-ditch at the hands of a poor-but-honest-not owner at Alexander Island in the same year of 1895. This plunger wasn't such a calcined tamale in those days as he is now, but he was some few, and he generally had enough up his sleeve in order to keep him in cigarettes and peanuts; which is to say that he had a winning way about him, and access to everything that was doing at that outlaw track. He dealt in jockeys quite a lot, giving them their figure with a slight scaling down, according to his own idea of what was coming to them for being kind to him. He was wise and he was haughty, and toward the wind-up of that Alexander Island season he fell into the notion, apparently, that things had to be done his way or the kickers fade out of the game.

"This poor owner that I'm talking about went on to Alexander Island with an ordinary bunch of sprinters, all except one filly, that was real good, but a bit high in flesh, and not ripe. It was a filly that could as a matter of fact beat anything at the track, being right and on edge, and she had the additional advantage of not being known all about. The poor owner has his own boy along with him, and he's pretty hard up. He sticks this filly in a six-furlong event, with the idea of really going after the purse, which he requires for expenses. He knows that the filly isn't right, but he dopes it that she can beat the lot pitted against her, anyhow, and he really means her to win. He tells his boy to take her right out in front and get as good a lead as he can, so that in case her flesh stops her the rest'll never be able to get near her. That's the arrangement right up until post time. The filly — well, suppose we call her Juliet — is not very well known at Alexander Island, and she has 5 to 1 against her.

"Now, it happens that this plunger knows all about Juliet being, as I say, a pretty fast proposition, but he doesn't think she can win in her condition, and, anyhow, he has something doing on another one in the race; he has so much doing in the race, in fact, that all the rest of 'em, except Juliet, are dead to the one he has picked to play. The plunger digs up the owner of Juliet and says to him:

" 'My son, your baby won't do to-day.'

" 'She'll make a stab, though,' said the owner. 'I need the cush, being several shy of paying my feed bills. The game has been throwing me lately. She's going to try.'

" 'You need the purse, hey?' said the plunger. 'That's not much money. Only $200, ain't it? How'd $500 do?'

" 'Spot coin?' asks the impecunious owner.

" 'Spot coin after my weanling gets the money.'

" 'You're on,' says the poor-but-honest-not owner. 'I'm not any more phony than my neighbors, but it's a case of real dig with me just now. Juliet'll finish in the ruck. Are you cinchy about the one you've got turning the trick?'

" 'It's like getting money in a letter,' says the plunger.

" 'All right,' says the poor owner, 'you can walk around to my stall and push me the five centuries after they're in.'

"The poor owner saw his boy, and Juliet's head was yanked off, with the boy's toes tickling her ears. She could have won in a walk, short of work as she was, but the boy had a biceps, and he held her down so that the plunger's good thing went through all right.

"After the race the plunger, who had made a great big thing out of it, hunted up the poor owner and beefed about the $500. He said that he hadn't been able to get as much money on his good one as he had expected and asked the poor owner to compromise for $300. The plunger's poor mouth doesn't tickle the poor owner a little bit, but he is a pretty foxy piece of work himself, and he takes the three hundred without letting on a particle that he thinks it a cheap gag. The plunger goes away thinking he has the poor owner on his staff for good, and the poor owner makes sundry and divers resolutions within himself, to the general effect that the next time he does business with that plunger he'll know it.

"Well, the poor owner doesn't race his good filly again for a couple of weeks, and all the time she's getting good. He gives her her work at about 3 o'clock every morning, in the dreamy dawn, so that nobody gets onto it just how good she is getting. He shoots her in about two weeks after he has been dickered down by the plunger. He knows that she's going to win, and with his other skates he has picked up nearly a thousand wherewith to play the Juliet girl to win. On the day before the race the plunger comes to him again.

" 'I see you've got that nice little girl of yours in to-morrow,' he says. 'How good is she?'

" 'She's got a show for the big end of it,' says the poor owner.

" 'Um,' says the plunger. 'Well, she'll only be at 5 to 1, whereas I've got a cinch in that that'll be as good as 15 to 1. Do you think we can do a little business?'

" 'On a strictly pay-in-advance basis, yes,' says the poor owner, chewing a straw. 'Maybe I'll be able to see my way to delivering the goods for a thousand down. Otherwise I win.'

"The plunger made a terrific beef, and tried persuasiveness, oiliness, bull-dozing the whole works, with the poor owner.

" 'Why,' he says, 'I can buy all the Juliets from here to Kentucky and back for a thousand.'

" 'Yes,' says the poor owner, 'but you can't shove a 15 to 1 shot through every day, either. Let's not talk about it any more. You've got my terms. Thousand down, right now, and Juliet will also run. No thousand, Juliet walks, and I'll get the coin anyhow by betting on her.'

"He got the thousand two hours before the race was run. The poor owner looked Juliet over, and called his boy into a dark corner of the stable.

" 'Take her out in front, son,' he said, 'and tow-rope them. Don't let 'em get within a block of you. I'll send your mother a couple o' hundred after you fetch her home.'

" 'She'd win with a dummy on her,' says the kid.

"Then the poor-but-honest-not owner takes the thousand he already has in his kick, and the thousand the beefing plunger has given him, and spraddles it all over the United States on Juliet at from 5 to 7 to 1.

"Juliet wins by fourteen lengths, and the plunger, with his mouth twitching, hunts

371

up the owner of Juliet. All he gets is a line of chile con carne conversation, and, finally, a puck in the eye.

" 'Do others or they'll do you' isn't the way they used to teach it when I went to Sunday-school," concluded the old-time trainer, "but there are occasions when the rule just has to be twisted that way."

THE SPIRITUALITY
OF THE HORSE

Those of us who remember 1974 were all aware of this story at the time. That was when farmers working in the Lintong District, Xi'an, Shaanxi province of China, uncovered what turned out to be an army of terra-cotta sculptures representing the military might of Qin Shi Huang, who was the first emperor of a unified China during 221–210 BCE. The purpose of this funerary was to guard the leader in the afterlife.

By the time excavations were completed, archaeologists had uncovered sculptures in three pits filled with in excess of 8,000 soldiers, as well as 520 horses and another 150 cavalry horses, plus chariots as well as other figures from acrobats to musicians.

I understand, now, that the horses were there not just to provide power and mobility to the troops of the afterlife. They were there for the courage, the heroic spirit they themselves represented. And let me tell you:

you look into the eyes of those figures and those horses seem alive.

Whatever your religious beliefs, there is no question that every living thing on the planet — indeed, in the universe — is connected. How attuned each of us is to that fact varies; but it doesn't alter that reality.

As with clergy, as with shamans, as with tai chi and kung fu masters, there is a connection that takes place which enriches all of the participants. This connection triggers a spiritual and energetic exchange, a positive zeitgeist that can impact not just the participants but, passively, any observers. At its most powerful, that bond can cause energetic and physical healing. Think of a simple, everyday example of a sick child and a puppy.

Many people say — not incorrectly — that they ascribe good health to a positive mental outlook, and a positive mental outlook to general satisfaction with their work, their family, their prospects. I certainly have been blessed with a job that challenges and thrills me every new day, a family that is close and loving, and a passion for horses.

For years, I have ascribed my health, this energy that I have, day after day, to the horses. That isn't to say the other parts of my life don't enrich me; they do, of course.

But the horse has an ancient soul, and I mean not just the strands of them that go back to LUCA but the ones that evolved from the eohippus, or "dawn horse," a foot-tall forebear that inhabited North America some sixty million years ago. Back then, humans were still basically lemurs. The pre-horse vegetarians, which fed on leaves, grasses, and shrubs, had to learn to run, and run fast, because they were prey. Think about it: we are talking about animals with instincts and senses that have been constantly refined for *sixty million years.*

We who ride are the beneficiaries of that unbroken chain of energy.

I have a business manager who used to caution me that owning horses was simply not cost-effective. He has stopped saying that. But he also looks at me and says, "It's all worthwhile." And it is. The horses have given me my health and energy, which is the basis of everything I do. It's the basis of what everybody does. And if you don't have your health, you won't have vitality, that inner energy, and you won't have your life.

Which is not to say, by the way, that one can only get this from horses. Actors know this well: we can, and should, get it from each other. Unfortunately, our world often puts us in adversarial positions with each other, which makes this difficult. Even our recreations become unhappily competitive. Sports, which put us in contact with vast amounts of energy, tend to be less about healthy competition than about winning. Boardrooms, where people should be pursuing a common goal, frequently become battlegrounds. Travel and you are increasingly apt to look over your shoulder rather than to open up and bond with another people or cultures. Encouraged by the Internet, we tend to form pockets of "us vs. them," whoever those pronouns may be.

Humans require healthy engagement and I am seeing less and less of that in the world around me.

It's both sad and funny that people and horses can usually settle their differences with relative ease. This morning I got out of my car when I was at the farm where I do most of my riding now, and one of my beautiful horses was tied up at a pole, and I went over, and I hugged the horse, and we had three minutes of communion in which I am holding this giant animal. It must be what a little child feels holding their father or a giant football player. I'm holding this horse, who is resting against me, and my whole being, my whole soul, is invested in the horse, and I can feel the breath of the horse, and I can feel the soul of the horse entering mine and mine entering it. It is a spiritual experience to be with those horses. And that's as invigorating, as inspiring as actually mounting the horse and doing some fun tricks on it.

This bonding is not just intimate, it's expansive. It's a shock wave but a healthy one that reaches out, and it lingers.

There's a country road that I take to get into this particular farm. It's a left-hand turn, and then there's a hundred-yard dirt road with a couple of houses to the left, and paddocks to the right with the horses in them. And the moment I make that left turn onto that dirt road, my spirit has already begun to *become* a horse. That doesn't mean I start acting equine. It means that power, rooted in prehistory, starts to fill my body, my soul. And when I drive up to the stable, which is the farthest end of this particular swath of land, I'm seeing my horses being readied for me. To my left, in a 300-by-600-foot arena, a huge arena, with the best footing possible, a clay base with sand and dirt on top, I'm seeing a couple of riders training my horses. And then my horse is ready for me. I don't have anything to do but walk from my car, a little stiff from the hour's ride, mount my horse, and move into that arena and join my friends and companions, some of whom are humans, most of whom are horses.

The stiffness is gone. Everything negative that might be lingering, hiding in body or mind is gone.

In this highly energized state, you have to be aware that you are open to negativity as well. The people who are there, in any arena — in any *life* situation — will put out emotion, exhaustion, unhappiness that may break the spell. There was a woman this morning who was really intruding in my connection. She was riding her horse over to Danny Gerardi, a genius trainer I mentioned earlier, and her hands were bad. And the horse's head was in the air, and she was so unhappy about herself and her horse that it filled the arena. And you want to tell her, "Be more gentle," but it's difficult. As much as one senses a ready bond, one also is sensitized to someone who is not, *will* not be open to any kind of camaraderie. You just have to redouble your efforts to remain open to your horse.

That is not too usual, even among professionals who ride with me. It might be like veteran actors who are doing the job, though they have lost the thrill of acting. They're performers, that's what they do to earn a living. And that's what some horse trainers are. I've always thought it would be interesting to find out how many people who ride horses think in terms of what I've just described. It's very private; even talking about it here I wonder how people will take what I'm saying.

It just occurred to me that if the crew of the *Enterprise* had encountered a planet where some ancient ascetic said he was "one" with his world, there would have been a wide spectrum of reactions. If we'd been there to tell him his planet was doomed, Kirk would have had to be convinced to let him stay so his released energy could join the exploded world as a small nebula or some such. We would, of course, have evacuated his exotic daughter.

I mention that because my own discoveries have been evolutionary. They have evolved from a feeling, to research, to increased understanding, to reading the books of Linda Kohanov and her teaching about the power of the herd and the spirituality of the horse, to my coming to this realization about this powerful, powerful transfer of energy at a submolecular, intangible level.

I don't know what stage of spiritualism I have reached. It's like religion, where you keep searching — or perhaps, more correctly, you don't so much search as remain open to subtle vibrations, to new connections. I truly don't know whether I'm at an end state and you don't go any further because here, in this world, a horse is an entity, a living entity, with its own biological needs and distractions. It has empathy and it has intelligence and it has a spirit with which you want to make a connection, but I cannot say whether "that's it" for now or whether this goes further and you realize that you can connect to whatever the horse is bonded with. We do that with our loved ones, to a degree; we feel what they feel, even if they aren't articulating it. We feel it very, very vaguely, through genetic memory, with our ancestors. The fight-or-flight reaction, for example.

I am very much like a horse in that respect; perhaps we all are. But we override our gut with our brain . . . not often to our advantage. A few examples.

I performed, once, with an orca . . . a killer whale. Maybe "performed" is too strong a word. I was present: Yaka did all the performing. I certainly didn't control that behemoth in any way.

It was 1987 at Marine World in Vallejo, California. I had finished *Star Trek IV: The*

Voyage Home, about a desperate effort to save the humpback whale. The appearance in Vallejo was to raise awareness for the California Rare and Endangered Species Preservation Program.

We were seeking publicity for an environmental cause, and the publicity people said, "We can get you to swim with this orca." And I've got pictures, by the way, on my wall. I'm looking at them right now.

While I was flying to the location, I was doing my homework and reading in the papers about the orca in San Diego that had gone down and half drowned the trainer. So I get there and the trainer of the orca says to me, "All right, this is very serious. Here's what we're going to do. You'll sit right here on the pier. You will open your legs and make a circle with your hands, and I'll whistle for the orca. The orca will come up and poke his head between your legs. You then step on his fins and put your arms around his nose so you'll have purchase and *stand* on his fins. He will then dance with you.

"Then when I blow the whistle again — and Bill, listen very carefully — I will have a fish in my hand. The orca will come to get the fish, and I want you, as swiftly and as silently as you can, to get up on the dock."

And that's how he said it. I've got pictures of me dancing with the orca. I've got pictures of me with the orca doing a jump, over me. You see me in the water and this B-17, this 747 of a killer whale going over my head and diving past me and into the water.

I was too busy not-drowning, not being overwhelmed by the waves this giant created, to worry about being attacked. But there was something else I felt, alone with the orca in that pool. Something I couldn't identify at the time. Since then I've read several books on orcas, and the captive ones are very angry at us. We have incarcerated them, and we've driven them insane, as we've driven all these animals in zoos insane. They're resentful and they're ready to kill us. And the trainers are very much aware of that.

Interestingly, the lower you go on the evolutionary chain in terms of creatures that are self-aware — at least, as far as we know — the sense of danger is of a different sort. The animal is simpler, reacting to hunger, reproductive needs, or self-preservation.

I did a movie in 1977 called *Kingdom of the Spiders,* with the wonderful, wonderful Woody Strode, in which killer tarantulas invade a small town. We used real tarantulas, and once you get past our own natural revulsion to small creatures that are tickly, crawly, and can get under loose-fitting clothes, tarantulas aren't as bad as people think.

Not that they're harmless. They'll sting you when threatened, and it'll hurt, but if you're careful how you handle them, they won't. Also, tarantula hair is used as itching powder. So they will make your skin crawl . . . literally. And the filmmakers used to dump bags of tarantulas over me.

My most vivid memory of that shoot was self-inflicted. I wanted to fall into the camera with a tarantula on my face, twitching my face, and then have the tarantula walk off. So it had to be live. It took me a half a dozen tries to glue it to my cheek, with just the right amount of glue and the correct amount of time to let it set; to fall into the camera, about two feet away; to give a dying twitch; and to have the tarantula walk off. It took me a half a dozen tries but I did it.

But there's a real difference between an animal that you can brush away, if you have to, and an orca. Or a bear. I remember, when I made *The Brothers Karamazov* with Yul Brynner in 1958, we had a scene with a big dancing bear. All I had to do was walk across the set — a tavern, as I recall. My insides were like a Geiger counter. Tick, tick, tick, TICK, TICK, tick tick . . . I thought it was my natural animal instinct for survival being triggered. It may have been, to some extent. And sometime after we shot that scene, I saw footage of that same bear turning on the person it was sitting beside and trying to eat that person. So I now believe it was the power of the bear that I felt. Fear is sudden: what I felt then was a slow build, peak, and ebb. Had I understood that, how much earlier I could have begun these explorations!

This brings us to something that is particularly interesting, though it's an area where I profess to be very much a novitiate. There are animal psychologists and also animal telepathists, psychics. I used one when my beloved Doberman pinscher had a disability in which his hindquarters were dragging. The veterinarians weren't able to find anything neural, so I went to an animal psychic, and she said that what the dog was telling me was that when I'd had him shipped the year before to do his breeding, they'd dropped the cage he was in.

Was the ailment traumatic or physical? Apparently both, since the former triggered the latter. Thereafter, whenever we took him anyplace, even by car, I took the time to comfort him, to reassure him that everything was all right. And slowly, his hindquarters regained their previous vigor. I read about another incident, which was corroborated, of a trainer in Indiana calling a psychic in California to say that they were having trouble with such and such a horse. The psychic said, "I am reading the horse, and the horse is telling me that the new fencing in my favorite spot in the pasture is making me nervous." It turned out that the horse had been shying from that spot for the last few days. It was something beyond a traditional, rational explanation, because this lady was saying to the guy two thousand miles away, "Here's what your horse is thinking." And the physical circumstances were correct.

I'm a bit of a psychic, too: I know what you're thinking. It's like a Vulcan mind meld. Mr. Spock used it to bond psychically with humans and even the Horta, a silicon-based alien. I know that Leonard took that process seriously. All you have to do is watch him seek the connection to understand that. Science is catching up to spiritualism more and more. It wasn't long ago that Chinese medicine was considered an outlier by establishment doctors. No longer. If I had to bet I would say that sooner rather than later psychic healing performed by highly sensitive individuals will be recognized as a legitimate form of therapy.

Until then, there is evidence of human-animal psychic transference, especially in animals like dogs and horses that are around humans a great deal. It is an area I personally hope to examine more in the future.

You know, you have to ask yourself whether maybe the pagans had something, whether there is a spirit in everything and it is a link to the godhead, however you call it, and whether what I am feeling will carry through with me to my death and perhaps beyond.

As I said, with some resignation, I don't know.

I *do* know that birds, in the thousands, turn like one in a flock. We know they do it because of slow-motion studies. Every bird, every fish in a school, is turning as one with the others. All those horses racing across the range turn left or right as one. They are highly aware of their environment and what's going on around them.

I also know it's a journey that I am on with these horses. I know that I am a far better rider, horseman, because of this spiritualism than I ever was when I was riding in movies like *White Comanche,* when it was more mechanical.

Leaving a stable, a farm, a ranch, is a very different experience than arriving. You do not feel a break in the same way that you experienced a sudden merging. When I cross that line again to go home, and I'm back on that road, I'm filled with goodness. If the morning has gone right, I'm filled with elation. I am filled with anticipation of going into competition. What I said earlier about people who want to win: I'm not nervous in competition, because that isn't my goal. I only want the beauty of this horse to be brought out. Which means I have to be at my best: if I make a mistake, this horse will do less well in the point spread. That won't be his fault, but mine. That's how good these horses are. As I said at the beginning of this book, they are Olympic athletes.

Yet after thirty-plus years as a serious rider, I firmly believe it goes deeper than this. There is a collective wisdom to horses and it appears that they have much more access to that than we do. It's a collective unconscious group mind that humans block because of our so-called practical mind — for example, the way we measure time, which is a major distraction — which animals are not subject to. The British writer and parapsychologist Rupert Sheldrake came up with the idea of the morphic resonance field for each species, the idea that when we die our experience is still retained by the collective morphogenic field of that particular species.

Many people who train horses empathically have had experiences where they connect with individual horses who are not present. They insist it is not a memory from their own experience, but it's coming through the horse. Native Americans who "skin walk" understand this idea very well.

It's a big, bold world out there . . . and we're only just beginning to grasp its incredible implications.

I can tell you, for myself, one of the beauties of riding is that the horse — well, I won't say he makes the job easy. Often, it isn't fun. But I have never, ever come from the experience empty-handed. And those experiences add up over the years, over the decades.

I have been privileged to make what one might describe as a fifty-year journey from Alpha Centauri on *Star Trek* to a spiritual Centaur in real life. To paraphrase a line I've heard . . . *somewhere:*

"It *is* . . . fun. Oh, my . . . !"

ABOUT THE AUTHOR

William Shatner has worked as a musician, producer, director, and celebrity pitchman, and notably played Captain Kirk on *Star Trek* from 1966 to 1969 and in seven Star Trek films. He won an Emmy and a Golden Globe for his role as attorney Denny Crane on the TV drama *Boston Legal*. He lives in Los Angeles with his wife, Elizabeth.

Jeff Rovin began his career as an editor for DC Comics. He has written nearly 150 books, as well as articles for *Ladies Home Journal, Omni,* and *Mad.* In addition to the *New York Times* bestselling *Tom Clancy's Op-Center* series, he wrote *A Vision of Fire*, with actress Gillian Anderson, and *Zero-G*, with Mr. Shatner. He lives in Manhattan with his wife, Victoria.

The employees of Thorndike Press hope you have enjoyed this Large Print book. All our Thorndike, Wheeler, and Kennebec Large Print titles are designed for easy reading, and all our books are made to last. Other Thorndike Press Large Print books are available at your library, through selected bookstores, or directly from us.

For information about titles, please call:
(800) 223-1244

or visit our website at:
gale.com/thorndike

To share your comments, please write:

Publisher
Thorndike Press
10 Water St., Suite 310
Waterville, ME 04901